P9-DEX-994

Live Large!

Affirmations for
Living the Life You Want
in the Body You Already Have

Cheri K. Erdman, Ed.D.

gürze books

Live Large!
Affirmations for Living the Life You Want
in the Body You Already Have
Cheri K. Erdman, Ed.D.
©1997; new Introduction ©2003 by Cheri K. Erdman

All rights reserved. Printed in the United States of America. No part of this
book, unless otherwise noted, may be used or reproduced in any manner
whatsoever without written permission of the publisher.

Gürze Books
PO Box 2238
Carlsbad, CA 92018
(800) 756-7533
www.gurze.com
Front cover design by Abacus Graphics, Oceanside, CA

Library of Congress Cataloging-in-Publication Data

Erdman, Cheri K.
Live large!: affirmations for living the life you want in the body you already
have / Cheri K. Erdman.
        p. cm.
Previously published: San Francisco : HarperCollins, c1997.
Previous pubication has subtitle: ideas, affirmations, and action for sane
living in a larger body.
Contains a new introduction.
    ISBN 0-936077-46-8 (alk. paper)
1. Overweight women — Mental health. 2. Self-esteem in women. 3. Body
image. 4. Obesity in women-Psychological aspects. I. Title.
RC552.025E729   2003
158'.1-dc22   2003018670

The authors and publishers of this book intend for this publication to
provide accurate information. It is sold with the understanding that it is
meant to complement, not substitute for, professional medical and/or
psychological services.

1 3 5 7 9 0 8 6 4 2

To the previous generations of strong women in my family; my mother, Dolores; my grandmother Nan; and my great-grandmother Katherine

CONTENTS

 Introduction

I am a fat woman, a woman of size and substance, a weighty woman, a woman who takes up space. I have been fat my entire life, except for those brief moments when I dieted my way into a not-fat body. I say "moments" because having a thinner body never lasted long. The second I stopped being ultra-vigilant about watching calories, my weight restored itself, plus a few extra pounds. I have made many attempts to change my naturally large body into an unnaturally thin one.

Many years ago I decided to stop dieting. I can't remember any specific event that propelled me to make this decision, no magic moment, no "aha" experience. I think I had just had it with food obsession controlling my thoughts and body hate controlling my moods. Anything, even the thought of forever remaining fat, seemed a better way to live than that. Besides, my weight wasn't getting in my way of having anything else I wanted. So why, I asked myself, should I continue to diet?

By establishing a normal relationship with food through a non-dieting lifestyle, I stepped away from the culture's expectations of me as a larger woman. I was throwing off the chains of always having to be "doing something about my weight" — which meant, of course, to always be on a diet.

The consequences of making this decision have been miraculous! I have done something about my weight: I've accepted it. And in my process of body-size acceptance I have learned many important lessons that I could not have learned if I had stayed in a dieting, body-hating mentality. The most important lesson of all, however, is this: I have the life I want in the body I already have. And so can you.

Live Large! brings a positive voice into your life and helps that voice become your very own. *Live Large!* supports you in your process of body-size acceptance no matter what your size or shape. *Live Large!* will help you change your mind to fit your body.

Because body-size acceptance is a slow, gradual, and individual process, *Live Large!* is written so that you aren't tied to a daily or even weekly calendar. Rather, *Live Large!* is organized so that you can take the time you need to absorb, reflect, and practice the message before moving on.

Each page is headed by a Big Idea — a word, phrase, or sentence that is important for you to consider in building size esteem.

The Big Idea is followed by an Affirmation. Affirmations are positive, affirming I-statements that reflect some thought or behavior you want to possess, and they are stated in the present tense of "I am" rather than in the future tense of "I will." Affirmations are important because with time and perseverance they will replace your negative, critical thoughts with positive, loving ones. Initially, saying your affirmations might feel like a useless exercise because you won't believe they are true. However, if you practice them with feeling and conviction in your thinking, writing, and speaking you will begin to believe them. Repeating our affirmations is a powerful way to counter the cultural messages that our worth is reflected in the size of our body.

After exploring the Big Idea in more detail, we will end with a Size-Wise Action. This action is designed to help you bring the Big Idea into your life so that you can live a productive and creative life as a woman of any size, without apology or shame.

Many of the Size-Wise Actions include a direct suggestion to write about your experience in your journal. Actually, I recommend journaling about all the Size-Wise Actions. For those of you who have not yet begun to keep a personal journal, now is a good time to start. Generally speaking, journal writing is a good way to keep track of your thoughts and feelings about your life. It provides a way of seeing yourself on paper, of being able to sort through the complexities of your life, of being able to go back in time to see how and why you have changed. For the purposes of *Live Large!* keeping a journal is very important because it will be a safe place to reflect on your process of body-size acceptance. It will help you find your own voice about your body, reflected in your own feelings, thoughts and words. It can become a source of support, comfort and even joy.

Live Large! is designed to be used in any way that fits you. If a Big Idea seems especially difficult for you right now, skip it and go on to another. You can also go back over the pages more than once since body-size acceptance is a spiraling process rather than a linear one. This means there may be times in which repeating, reflecting and practicing a Big Idea for a second, third or fourth time can be beneficial in continuing to support your effort at building self-acceptance and size esteem. You are the expert on your body and on your process of size-acceptance, so use this book accordingly.

If you need more specific information about the topics presented in *Live Large!* I recommend reading my first book, *Nothing To Lose: A Guide to Sane Living in a Larger Body*, or any of the books listed in the Resources section at the end of *Live Large!* These works will provide you with the necessary research and information related to body-size acceptance. To give you a foundation for using *Live Large!* until you have done further reading, I have included a few major points related to building size-acceptance and self-esteem below:

- The research studies that say health is always related to weight are tainted by a science that cannot see past its own bias against fat. Furthermore, these studies are almost always conducted by obesity researchers who may have a conflict of interest, especially if they are consultants to pharmaceutical companies that are developing diet drugs or have financial ties to the diet industry. In other words, don't always believe what you read or hear about weight and health in the media.

- There is ample evidence that a person can be "fat and fit."

- A growing number of professionals in the nutrition, exercise, psychological and medical fields are using a new approach to health and wellness called Health at Every Size (HAES). HAES is built on respect for all people of all sizes and believes that everyone in entitled to be as healthy as he or she can be — regardless of weight.

The HAES approach includes the following behaviors:

- Eat for your health as well as your pleasure by paying attention to your body's internal signals of hunger and satiety. (Stop dieting!)

- Become physically active as a way to enjoy yourself and increase health benefits regardless of weight loss. (Go for a walk!)

- Get on with your life no matter what you weigh. Putting off doing what you want until you lose weight is a loss of precious time that can never be regained. (Act on your dreams now!)

- Body-size acceptance is a process. In other words, it is almost impossible to decide to accept your body and then never have to do anything else about that decision. The reality is that as long as we live in a weight-phobic society we will receive negative messages from the culture. We need to be aware of these messages and the impact they have on our thinking, feeling and behaving — and then remind ourselves of our right to be happy and healthy in the bodies we already have.

– Support is crucial in the process of building size-acceptance. Support can come in many forms from reading books and articles that support a HAES philosophy (and stop subscribing to magazines that make you feel bad about yourself!), to befriending other women who are trying to get over weight obsession, to buying clothes that fit you today (and getting rid of those in your closet that don't!), to starting your own support group.

– Begin to view yourself as a whole person, not just a physical being. Pay attention to your emotional, intellectual and spiritual self as well as your body. Remember, you have a body . . . and you are more than your body!

These ideas complement what you will find in *Live Large!* which provides you with a flexible structure for working through your own individual process of body-size acceptance.

My wish for you is that you learn how to have the life you want in the body you already have.

I hope you decide to *Live Large!*

Part 1

initiation

Self-esteem can't be weighed or measured

How much do you think self-esteem weighs? Self-esteem has nothing to do with numbers. It can't be measured by dress sizes, fat calipers, hours of exercise, or fat grams. Self-esteem has *everything* to do with how you choose to perceive yourself. Will you choose to perceive yourself as a good person who feels good about herself regardless of her weight, her dress size, or other people's opinions of her body? Or will you choose to perceive yourself as "bad" because scales, dress sizes, and other people's opinions about your size rule your life? You have the power to choose your perception. Will you have high self-esteem or low self-esteem? The decision is yours.

affirmation

I am a good person and I feel good about myself.

size-wise action

Practice putting away your judgements about size and weight. If the numbers on the scale throw you in a panic, don't weigh yourself. If the size of your dress bothers you, cut the label out of the garment. Quit playing the self-esteem numbers game and practice feeling good about yourself based on who you are.

❧ *Healthy bodies come in all sizes*

Assume that you are unhealthy because you are over the numbers on the height-weight chart? Do you believe your health to be bad just because your weight exceeds our society's ideal? It's time to quit making assumptions about your health based on these standards and start assuming responsibility for your health based on your own body truths and body wisdom. Keep in mind that having a thin body does not guarantee a life free of health concerns, nor does being fat translate into a life full of health problems. It *is* possible to be a large *and* healthy person. Adopt a lifestyle committed to health rather that weight loss.

affirmation

I have a large and healthy body.

size-wise action

Imagine how your life would be different if you believed that people of all sizes could be healthy. Rather than relying on the old "answer" of dieting, what else could you do today to take responsibility for your health as a larger person? Now do it!

❦ *The dictionary defines large as greater than average*

Words have a powerful effect on our lives. They can create a mood, state of mind, a reality. Pay attention to the words you use to describe yourself and others. The words you choose can alter how you feel, what you think, and even the very truth of your existence. If you aren't comfortable describing yourself as fat because of the word's negative connotation, then try using softer words to describe your body: *large, voluptuous, curvaceous, great, round, full, big, ample, substantial, Rubenesque*. Use the power of words to positively define your reality as a larger woman.

affirmation

I am greater than an average woman.

size-wise action

Think of being large as also being strong, being substantial, having weight in the world, having weight to throw around, thinking big, and being big-hearted. Think of other positive ways you can define your reality as a larger woman with the power of your words. Write these in your journal.

❧ *A large number of woman are large*

In this country alone there are more than thirty million larger women. And the average dress size in the United States is a size fourteen, not a size six. Let's face it: we are not a minority, although people treat us as though we were. It's easy to fall into feeling rejected or become an easy target for discrimination and harassment if you feel like you're the only one. You aren't. Can all thirty million of us be lazy, stupid, ugly, sloppy, uncontrollable, unhappy, unhealthy, unlovable, and undisciplined? I don't think so. So take pride in our numbers. Take pride in yourself.

affirmation

I am part of a network of beautiful, worthwhile, productive, size-accepting women.

size-wise action

Pay attention to all the large women you see in one day. Allow yourself to feel connected to each large woman you encounter. If you feel moved to do so, look her in the eye and give her a reassuring smile that says you notice her. Write about this experience in your journal.

❦ *Fat people are fat for a variety of reasons*

The world sees fat people as if we were cracked out of the same egg. Our culture thinks that all fat people are fat because we eat too much and exercise too little—in short, because we lack self-control, discipline, and willpower. This is untrue. Fat people are fat for a variety of reasons, the most important being genetics. Some of us have been born with the obesity gene, making it hard for us to be thin no matter what we eat, how stringently we diet, or how much we exercise. So give back the culture's interpretation of fat people, and reclaim your own body truths.

affirmation

I am a unique individual.

size-wise action

Find photographs of your relatives—your mother, father, aunts and uncles, grandparents. Look at their body types. Do any of their bodies resemble yours? Feel proud of your body and how it connects you to your heritage. Write about this in your journal.

❦ *Body size is unrelated to the quality of a person's life*

How often have you awakened, looked in the mirror, and begun your day by criticizing your body? How often have these thoughts infiltrated and poisoned your mood and your day? How often have these thoughts stopped you from having the kind of life you really want? Well, good news is here! There is more than one way to construct the truth about the size of your body. One way is to remind yourself that the size of your body isn't important in determining the quality of your life. Remember, there are plenty of *happy fat* people as well as plenty of *unhappy thin* people. Having a good life is connected to the size of your heart and mind, not the size of your body.

affirmation

I have the life I want in the body I already have.

size-wise action

Practice this: Get up in the morning and look at your reflection in the mirror with kind of gentle eyes. Remind yourself that your body is a *vehicle* for you to live your life, not the center of your life! Enlarge your mind and heart. Accept your body.

🌷 An "ideal" body does not guarantee a happy life

There are all kinds of people in the world living in all kinds of bodies. It doesn't make sense that only people with ideal bodies are happy. In fact, research on women's body image shows that women with ideal bodies are often the most preoccupied with them—how to keep them in shape, how to feed them without gaining weight, how to stop them from aging. They treat their bodies as if they were objects—not just to others but to themselves as well! This is not the road to a joyful, happy life. This is the path to obsession, guilt, and shame. Taking appropriate care of our bodies, regardless of their size, is one way to a happier life.

affirmation

I choose joy and happiness in my life.

size-wise action

When you're in a group of women who are talking negatively about their bodies, try changing the subject or walking away. Monitor what you say about your body. Make sure only the most respectful remarks leave your lips. Talk about your body with dignity and joy.

✿ Replace diet obsession with increased self-awareness

How much time have you spent thinking about food and diets? Instead, consider using that time to discover ways of increasing your self-awareness. Learn more about yourself. What do you like to do in your free time? What are your favorite colors, music, foods, fantasies, authors, cars, dreams? What kind of people do you like to be with? What subjects do you want to know more about? Which places have you always longed to visit? What kinds of experiences do you dream of having? These are worthy thoughts and actions for building a rewarding and fulfilling life. Dieting isn't.

affirmation

I am willing to expand my self-awareness

size-wise action

Every time you are tempted to think about dieting today, replace the thought with this: What does my fantasy life look like? What can I do right now that will make my life today a part of my fantasy life?

 *Ample*

A mple is a lovely word. It means "of great size, amount, extent, or capacity." When someone or something is described as ample, there is a hint of fullness and magnitude. Ample is one way—a positive way—to describe the body of a woman of size. Ample can also describe the space a woman fills with her mind and spirit. Ample women need to balance their ample bodies with spacious minds and soaring spirits, taking up space in all parts of their lives, living with breadth and range. Think about being enough, filled to capacity with your life. Practice being ample not only in body, but also in mind and spirit.

affirmation

I am ample in body, mind, and spirit.

size-wise action

Imagine your life as an ample opportunity to express your larger self. What would you be doing that you are not doing now? Fill up the space of your life. Do one of those things today.

❦ *Curves are more inviting than straight lines*

A curved line on a piece of paper appeals to our creativity; it invites the eye to follow it and the mind to wonder where it will go next. A straight line, on the other hand, is direct, to the point, leaving nothing to the imagination, going from here to there. A curving body is like a curved line in a work of art. Artists over the centuries have chosen to paint rounded bodies; following the lines of the hip, the breast, and the buttocks keeps the eye interested and the mind intrigued: what is around the next bend? That is the kind of body a larger woman has—rounded, curvaceous, gently rolling, falling up and down, soft. That is the kind of body you have. Look at your body through the eyes of an artist. See why your body is a work of art.

affirmation

I am a soft, curvaceous, rounded woman.

size-wise action

Collect art that depicts women with soft, curvaceous lines. Look at these women often. Understand that you are just as beautiful. Write about this in your journal.

A healthy body is the best body to have

Over the centuries fashion has dictated hundreds of different looks. One era endorsed the rounded, pregnantlike belly as fashionable. In contrast, we now demand flat stomachs within weeks of giving birth! In other times, the full-bodied Rubenesque woman was glorified, while now we exalt the thin-bodied skeletal woman. When are we going to throw off the whims of fashion designers and reclaim the right to decide what is "fashionable" for our bodies? Make the decision to include health as a permanent part of your fashion wardrobe—regardless of what designers say your body should look like this year.

affirmation

I treat my body with respect.

size-wise action

Read the history of women's body image. Look at the pictures and the drawings that record the fickleness of fashion. What's *in* today will be *out* tomorrow. Be "in" all the time by redefining what being fashionable means to you: being healthy!

Self-esteem

Self esteem is getting big press these days. It is the topic of books and the subject of school curricula. Debated by liberals and conservatives, it is the darling of a new wave of humanism. Self-esteem can make or break a person's ability to have a rewarding, fulfilling existence. Self-esteem is the evaluation we give ourselves regarding who we are. Self esteem for larger women can be precarious because we have bodies that are not valued by the culture and therefore often not valued by ourselves. If we connect all our self-esteem with our bodies, we are in big trouble indeed. Build your self-esteem by placing value on all parts of yourself, not just your body.

affirmation

I think of myself as worthwhile and acceptable.

size-wise action

How do you rate your self-esteem? What part does your body play in your self-esteem? How can you focus on the other parts of yourself, the parts that you view as positive? Write about these things in your journal.

❧ *Increased self-awareness increases size acceptance*

Becoming an emotionally healthy person will help you become a healthy person overall. Increasing your self-awareness is a necessary part of increasing your body-size acceptance because the two are interrelated and inner-connected: what you know about yourself influences how you choose to behave and perceive yourself. Increasing your self-awareness requires a fair amount of time, tuning into yourself and what you think, feel, and do. It can happen in several ways: through therapy, support groups, asking others for feedback, reading, and reflecting in your journal. If you really want to change how you feel about your body, then make a commitment to increase your self-awareness.

affirmation

I am self-aware, especially in my body-mind connection

size-wise action

How do you learn about yourself best? Through talking with someone, or by reading, reflecting, and writing? Make a commitment to increase your self-awareness by choosing the method that works for you. Then do it.

❧ *Body-wise expert*

With so much conflicting information floating around about body size, fat, health, exercise, and dieting, is it any wonder that women are confused about their health? Here's my solution: While the experts are battling it out— should we diet or not? does additional weight pose health risks? what percentage of fat intake is healthiest? how important are exercise and fitness? who's at risk and who isn't?—*we still have to live our lives*. Become the expert on your own body, and make decisions about it and your health accordingly. No one else knows more about what's best for you.

affirmation

I am the expert when it comes to my own body.

size-wise action

Begin to pay attention to your body and its need to eat, move, play, rest, work, breathe. Practice eating *what* your body really wants *when* you are physically hungry, moving when and how your body wants to move to feel energized, playing when you need to balance working, and resting when your body is tired. And always, always remember to *breathe*!

🌷 *Everybody has a different body*

Remember the old saying "Variety is the spice of life"? Think of your body, with its unique shape, size and coloring, as one of the many in the spice rack of life. Imagine how boring food would taste without the spices we add to enhance flavors. Now imagine how boring it would be to look out into the world and see everybody in exactly the same body. There would be no room for imagination and curiosity, because what you look like would be what everyone else looks like. Ho-hum. Gray. Flat. Flavorless. No way! It's wonderful that everybody has a different body because variety perks up the landscape, gives us something interesting to look at, something to be curious about. It fires up our imaginations. Be grateful that your body is not like everyone else's. Be grateful that your body is yours.

affirmation

I appreciate my distinctively different body.

size-wise action

What kind of spice does your body remind you of? Hot pepper, flavorful basil, tangy ginger, exotic cinnamon, fragrant vanilla? Make a connection with your body in a spicy way.

❦ *Your body is made to move*

Exercise has long been used as punishment for being fat, so, understandably, most larger people avoid exercise. Moreover, fat people who do exercise are likely to be ridiculed about their size. All this makes it tough to begin, but you must. Being connected to your body through movement helps build a positive relationship between you and your body. And this builds self-esteem. Research shows that exercise affects our fitness level and health more than it does our weight. So commit to your health instead of to weight loss, and you'll soon discover how enjoyable moving your body can be!

affirmation

Today I choose to move my body in pleasurable ways.

size-wise action

Go for a walk and focus on nature's beauty. Do not time your walk, or mark your distance, or take your pulse, or tell yourself that you will walk five miles a day from now on. Just walk until you feel pleasantly refreshed, relaxed. Think about doing it again sometime soon. Remind yourself often how pleasant it is to walk.

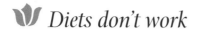 *Diets don't work*

Since the 1920's more than 26,000 diets have been marketed in the United States. If any of these diets worked, do you think there would be a fat person left today? Diets fail us 95 percent of the time. Yet the diet industry keeps pumping out new ways for us to shed pounds, blaming us for lack of willpower instead of putting the blame where it belongs—on the ineffectiveness of dieting. It's time for all women to stop dieting. It's time for us to start trusting our own body wisdom in choosing foods for health and pleasure. The next time you are tempted to diet, just stop and remind yourself that a diet has never worked before. What makes you think it will work now?

affirmation

I choose healthful foods to eat based on my body wisdom.

size-wise action

Make a list of all the diets you've tried and the amount of money you've spent on them. Include diet products, services, programs, even therapy. Now add it up. Next, think of how much you weighed when you went on your first diet and how much you weigh now. Get mad! Remind yourself of these facts when you are tempted to diet again.

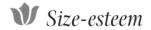 *Size-esteem*

When you combine *size acceptance* with *self-esteem*, you get SIZE-ESTEEM: feeling really, really good about yourself in your body. You will reach this "feeling good" place when you have accepted your body size and shape. Size-esteem means being proud of your body, regardless of its size. Size-esteem means taking care of your body, regardless of its size. Size-esteem means having what you want, regardless of your size. Size-esteem means getting what you earn, regardless of your size. Decide to feel good about yourself and your size. Decide to live with size-esteem.

affirmation

I feel good about my size.

size-wise action

What are some of the advantages of a having larger body? List these in your journal. This is the place from which to begin building size-esteem. Add to your list often as a way of reminding yourself that you feel good about being a larger women.

Part 2

inspiration

 *Largesse*

The word largesse means "gifts bestowed" as well as "generosity of spirit or attitude." Learn how to apply this word (and other fat-positive words) in your life as an affirmation of being large. What could be positive about being large, you ask? Many things! But we've spent so much time hating our bodies, we haven't looked around to notice the good things, such as having more presence, having weight in the world, being strong, being substantial, being big-hearted, being powerful. There are many more fat-positive realities, but learning how your weight has served you is a personal journey. Begin to see how being large is a positive thing in your life. Appreciate your size.

affirmation

I am a gifted and generous woman.

size-wise action

Go to a quiet place, close your eyes, and relax. Ask yourself, "what gifts does my larger body bring into my life?" From this quiet place allow an answer to come. Accept this answer even if you don't agree with it. Write about this experience in your journal.

❦ *Size acceptance is a personal process*

There will always be people who feel they have a right to tell you how to live your life. And when it comes to accepting your body, some of them will tell you *in absolute terms* how it should be done. This is a trap. Learning to accept your body is a very personal process, one you need to discover on your own. A multitude of factors including biology, standards of appearance, health concerns, family background, eating and dieting patterns, life dreams, and available energy do need to be addressed—by you. So take responsibility for the journey. It's your body and your life.

affirmation

I am in charge of my process to accept my body.

size-wise action

The next time you are tempted to buy someone else's program designed to change your life, stop! Remember, that person is not the one who has to get up every day and live in your body. *You* are! Take responsibility for your life in the body you already have.

🌿 *There is beauty in diversity*

Learning to appreciate the beauty and diversity in all body types is an important step in the process of body-size acceptance. We have to learn to stretch our definition of beauty to include images of all women, not just those who grace the covers of fashion magazines, billboards, and TV screens. We can do this by making a conscious effort to include images of beautiful *large* women in our daily lives. Looking through the pages of *Radiance* or *BBW* is a start. At first, seeing larger women as beautiful may feel uncomfortable. In time, however, you will begin to see that big or small, fat or thin, *all* women are beautiful!

affirmation

I see beauty in myself and in every woman I meet.

size-wise action

When you are out enjoying the beauty of nature, notice this: Are all the flowers, trees, birds, and clouds exactly the same? Isn't the hearty sunflower as beautiful as the delicate lily-of-the-valley? Relate this idea to the beauty of women and write about it in your journal.

Compulsive eating and size are not related

When people see a fat woman they automatically think she eats too much. This is *not* necessarily true. Studies show that the food intake of the lean and the fat is similar. Studies also show that there is no relationship between a person's size and the probability that she has an eating disorder. There is, however, a relationship between *dieting* and having an eating disorder. So, before you buy into the myth that all fat people eat too much, or that all fat people have an eating disorder, think about this: dieting turns people into compulsive eaters; dieting makes people fatter. If you have been a chronic dieter, you have probably been (or are) a compulsive eater. Stop dieting and begin to develop a natural relationship with food again. And let your weight take care of itself.

affirmation

I eat in a natural, healthful way.

size-wise action

If you have trouble with compulsive eating, please refer to the "Resources" at the end of *Live Large!*

 *Miracles*

Dieting plans say (or imply) that they are the miracle cure for being "overweight" or that losing weight is a miracle. Or that someone's life was miraculously saved when she lost hundreds of pounds. Actually, losing weight and *keeping it off for more than three years* is a kind of miracle— only 2-5 percent of the people who diet can do this. But the miracle of the body encompasses more than losing weight. The real miracle is called life, and you are already living that miracle in the body you inhabit right now. Another miracle occurs when you respond to your body based on its own needs, not someone else's imposed needs. In other words, if you eat what your body wants when it is hungry, if you exercise your body when it needs to be moved, if you rest when your body is tired, or work and play when your body has energy, you are a living, moving miracle. Your body is a miracle.

affirmation

My body is a living, moving miracle

size-wise action

Today, give thanks often for the miracle of your body.

❦ *Make it up as you go along*

When we decide to enter the territory of size acceptance, we take a big step into a relatively unknown area. After all, few women have been there before us; there are not many role models to call upon for stories about their process. So, we have to fortify ourselves with the courage to be different, trust in our own process, and seek a childlike sense of discovery. We begin this journey without really knowing how to get there, or even what "there" looks like. How do we do this? By making it up as we go along! Each day will provide us with opportunities to choose over and over again how we will perceive our bodies, how we will feed our bodies, how we will treat our bodies. Courage. Trust. Discovery. Opportunities. What more do we need?

affirmation

I make decisions about my body based on my personal experience and body wisdom

size-wise action

Listen to your body and create your process of making peace with your body day by day, decision by decision.

🌿 *Support is as essential as air*

Just as you need air to live, if you are in the process of accepting your body size, you need support. It is difficult, if not impossible, to go about this process without having someone or something cheering you on. Support can come in all sorts of packages—friends, family members, books that offer the viewpoint that you can be large and healthy, magazines on size acceptance such as *Radiance* and *BBW*, or organizations such as the National Association to Advance Fat Acceptance (NAAFA), movement programs designed especially for larger women, beautiful clothes that fit, art that depicts larger women as beautiful, and so on. Go out and get the support you need, and take it in like a breath of fresh air.

affirmation

I support myself as a woman of size.

size-wise action

Find one friend you can talk to about size acceptance who will just listen (no advice!). Or join a discussion group with like-minded women. Begin to build a support network that works for you.

🌷 *Positive self-talk*

Self-talk is what we say about ourselves to ourselves. You know, that little voice that is our companion on life's journey? Well, that little voice can be a big influence in your life. It just depends on what your voice is saying to you about you. Does your self-talk include congratulations for the outrageously wonderful and fabulous things you've done? Or does your self-talk fill your mind with criticism and nagging at every turn? Tune in. What are you saying to yourself right now? Is it something like, "Well, I've never done anything outrageously wonderful and fabulous, so no wonder I never congratulate myself"? If it is, stop! Change what you say to yourself *about* yourself. Undermine the negative messages with positive ones: "I am outrageously wonderful and fabulous." Soon you will be-if you aren't already!

affirmation

I talk to myself about myself in the most positive ways.

size-wise action

Monitor your self-talk. Write down the negatives. Replace them with positive responses. Train your self-talk to be you best friend and cheerleader.

❦ *The dictionary defines fat as productive, rich, plentiful, fertile, abundant, and abounding in desirable elements*

Language is a funny thing. Words start out having one meaning and then, because of changes in the cultural context, begin to mean something else. The word *fat* used to reflect a positive state of being rich, prosperous, lucrative, full. But since we've started living in a "no fat" world, fat (including the word itself) is seen as being bad, embarrassing, shameful. Reclaim the original meaning of the word *fat*. Think of yourself as ample, desirable, abundant, prosperous. You wouldn't mind having a fat bank account, would you? Then why would you mind having a fat body?

affirmation
I am an abundant and desirable woman.

size-wise action
Practice using the word *fat* whenever you can. Say it aloud to yourself, or occasionally refer to yourself as a fat woman and notice the reaction. Practice saying fat until you can say it without embarrassment or shame.

Fat people experience good health when they live in cultures where their size is not stigmatized

Cross-cultural studies of societies in which no stigma attaches to size have found that fat people in those societies are quite healthy. They show no evidence of the "high risk" factors sometimes associated with being fat in North America. These findings prompt us to ask whether it is the *stress* of living in a fat-phobic culture, rather that being fat itself, that makes some fat people unhealthy.

affirmation

I am a large and healthy person.

size-wise action

Take care of your body as if it were the culture's perfect size. Find yourself a size-friendly physician, if you do not have one already. See your doctor for a yearly physical, as well as when you have health problems. Do not avoid going to the doctor because of your weight. Begin to separate your weight from your health.

Listen to your body

The medical industry interprets larger people's body size through a disease model and prescribes dieting as the cure for our "disease." This prescription rarely works for us. We know from experience that dieting makes us temporarily thinner and permanently fatter. Are we to believe the medical and diet industry on our own body truths? We have been taught to mistrust our bodies, to see them as our enemies. They are not. We must learn to listen to the voice and language of our own bodies. Pay attention! Your body is telling you something right now. Are you listening?

affirmation

I am wise about my health because I listen to my body.

size-wise action

Stop, close your eyes, and tune into your body. How does it feel? Tired? Energized? Hungry? Warm? Content? Tingly? What? Move your awareness into your legs, arms, trunk, neck, shoulders, head. What message is your body giving your right now? Learn to listen to your body's voice. Your body has a language of its own.

 Breathe!

Breathing is the essential element of living. When there is no breath, there is no life. Normally we don't think about breathing—we just do it, in and out, automatically. Your breath, however, is more than a way to give you the oxygen you need to live. Your breath is your connection to your mind and body, your connection to your soul. Breathing goes beyond body size. Learn to breathe deeply to relax your body, quiet you mind, and connect to yourself in deeper ways.

affirmation

I connect with myself through my breath. (Now breathe!)

size-wise action

Stand straight, shoulders back, knees slightly bent. Relax your abdomen, letting your stomach hang. Inhale and fill your chest with air. Feel your ribs expand. Imagine that you inhale the words *body acceptance*. Then exhale the words *body-hate*. Write about this in your journal.

♥ *My body, my business*

There may have been times when someone else thought she or he knew what was best for you and your body. This advice may have come from well-meaning family members, from your doctor, or from your best friend. OR it may have come abruptly from a stranger on the street or an ad on TV. Everyone has an opinion about what fat people should do (diet) and what they should look like (thin). Your body is no one else's business. It is private matter. Only you arc in charge of your body.

affirmation

I am in charge of my body.

size-wise action

If someone tries to talk to you about your weight in a way that is shaming or inappropriate, be assertive. Firmly tell her or him that your body is your own personal business. Tell that person to pay attention to her or his own body not yours.

 *Dignity*

It's amazing how many people feel they have the right to comment on someone else's body or appearance. If you are a woman of size, you are probably no stranger to the hostility some people feel about fat. An aggressively unkind remark can be made anywhere—on the street, in the grocery store, at a restaurant, in the gym, on the beach, even in your own home. Sometimes it feels like no place is safe from the hostility of fat phobia. What can you do if you are verbally assaulted about your weight or appearance? Stick up for yourself! Have a response ready in your mind for times like these, and choose if and when to use it. Try a response like, "You should be ashamed of yourself for talking to me like that!" Or, "My body, my business!" You deserve to be treated with respect, regardless of the size of your body.

affirmation

I deserve to be treated with respect and dignity.

size-wise action

If you are going someplace where a comment is likely to be made about your weight, prepare yourself with responses. Practice them with a friend until you become comfortable standing up for yourself.

❧ *Body truths*

The culture conspires to snatch away our personal experiences of our bodies by telling us *how* our bodies should be and what they should look like. Every day we are bombarded with the message that our bodies do not match up with the culture's idea of perfection. Your body has its own shape, size, biology, rhythms, coloring, and genetics, and it carries your unique life experiences. Your body has its own truths, which may be different from the culture's truths. Respect your body and its truths, even if the culture doesn't.

affirmation

My experience of my body is my own truth.

size-wise action

What are your truths about your body? For one day, practice paying attention to your body and its rhythms. Look at your size, shape, and coloring without society's judgment. Think about your family's bodies and your genetic connection to them. Contemplate your body's truths.

❤ *Body-size acceptance is slow and gradual*

Because there is so much pressure to conform to the culture's ideal regarding body size, it may take a while for you to reach a comfortable level of accepting your body. Body-size acceptance, because it often comes slowly and gradually, may at first seem like an impossible goal. Be patient with yourself and your process. Each day is a gift when you allow yourself to become involved in your life without body obsession controlling your thoughts. Give yourself this gift one day at a time.

affirmation

My body is the perfect size for me right now.

size-wise action

Pretend for one day that you are not a larger women. Pretend that you are the culture's "ideal" size. Go about your day acting as if you have this smaller body. Notice what you do, and write about it in your journal.

❦ *You can have the life you want in the body you already have*

Many women live by this rule: when I lose weight I will (pick one): a. get into a relationship, b. buy beautiful, expensive clothes, c. change careers, d. (fill in the blank), e. all of the above. If you are one of these women, try this rule instead: "TODAY I will do what pleasures me *regardless* of what I weigh." Your weight has nothing to do with your ability to have the perfect life for you. It is your mind and its belief system about your weight that dictate what you will have or not have in your lifetime. So begin to change your mind about your body. Imagine the perfect life for you. Now go out and do something today to make that life a reality.

affirmation

I am living the perfect life for me right now.

size-wise action

Make a list of all the things you are waiting to do until you have lost weight. Now go through your list and pick one thing that you are willing to do *now*, without having lost a pound. When you have accomplished that, pick another. You'll be amazed. Soon you'll be living the life you've always wanted in the body you already have.

❦ *Low body-weight doesn't guarantee high self-esteem*

Advertising leads us to believe that young, thin, beautiful people are the happiest and have the highest self-esteem. This is not always the truth. Advertising depends on making all of us feel insecure about ourselves—even the young, thin, and beautiful! Self-esteem cannot be bought with diets and thinner bodies. It must be earned by learning to accept and love ourselves in the bodies we already have (yes, even larger bodies). One study showed that larger women who stopped dieting and accepted their body size had higher self-esteem than those who didn't. Get the message? Develop high self-esteem by accepting and loving yourself exactly as you are today.

affirmation

I increase my self-esteem by expressing my value in the world as a woman of size.

size-wise action

Stop weighing your self-esteem by weighing yourself on the scale. Self-esteem based on numbers is fleeting and not a true measure of your worth. In your journal keep track of how you feel about kicking the "weighing in" habit.

 *Spirit*

Spirit has been defined in a variety of ways—as essence, vitality, creation. Spirit reflects the connection we feel toward something larger than ourselves. Spirit is important in the lives of larger women because it allows us to transcend the pain of being fat by turning that pain into an expression of our meaning and purpose. Larger women can do this by living our lives in terms of connection and action: spirit in action. So recognize that the essence of you is not defined by your size, that the vitality you possess can be larger than life, and that the creation of all you desire is at your fingertips!

affirmation

I am a spiritual being inhabiting a physical body.

size-wise action

Discover your creativity! Paint, garden, write in your journal, put on your favorite music and dance. Express the larger part of you. Put your spirit into action and see what kind of life you can create.

 *Entitlement*

Entitlement is having a right to or making a claim on something. You, as a larger woman, are entitled (just like women who wear a size 8) to do whatever you want with your life and have whatever you desire. Having a bigger body or a smaller body has nothing to do with it. What is required, though, is that you first *believe* you are entitled, then act on that belief. Bring entitlement out of the back reaches of your mind. You have a right to the life you want in the body you already have. Make a claim on that life by focusing on getting what you want out of your life rather than focusing on the size of your body.

affirmation

I am entitled to the life I want.

size-wise action

Think of someone you know who takes her or his entitlement seriously. Think about that person's behavior. What do you notice that you are willing to let rub off on you? Now act as if you are entitled. Practice making a claim on your life and see what happens.

🌢 *Fat women have nonconforming bodies*

For years, many of us have been trying to do all the right things (diet and exercise), only to get the "wrong" results (staying fat or getting even fatter). Our experience has shown us that our bodies do not cooperate with the prescriptions of doctors and exercise gurus. We are now ready to think about our nonconforming bodies in a new and different way: they will never become what they *are not* no matter how hard we try, so they must be what they are—naturally big, round, soft, curvaceous, full beautiful bodies. Our bodies conform to what they are regardless of what society says they should be. They always have. They always will.

affirmation

My body conforms to its own biology, rhythms, hunger, size, shape, and experiences.

size-wise action

Throw away your scale. Your body knows how much it needs to weigh. So trust your body, even if it's a nonconforming one!

❦ *The mirror lies*

What we see in the mirror is not based on reality. The mirrored body image reflects our perceptions—perceptions that are tainted with our culture's judgement of fat people. How others see us is also an individual perception based on *their* judgments about body size. So you see, there is no reality, just perception. You can choose to see yourself in the mirror in a variety of ways: as a large woman who is "disgustingly huge" and needs to exert some willpower and control over herself; or as a large woman who is acceptable, lovable, and beautiful. What will your mirror reflect back to you today?

affirmation

I see myself as acceptable, lovable, and beautiful.

size-wise action

Find some time when you can be alone, and treat yourself to a leisurely hot bath. When you are re-laxed, go to a full-length mirror and look at yourself. Soften your eyes as you do this, and begin to see yourself and your body without judgment and shame. Practice this until you can say that you are acceptable, lovable, and beautiful.

❦ *Dieting and size acceptance make strange bedfellows*

It is difficult, if not impossible, to accept our bodies when we are dieting for weight loss. Dieting, as a concept and in practice, implies restricting food intake for the express purpose of losing weight. How can you be trying to lose weight, hence changing your body size, and at the same time be trying to accept your body as it is? These two behaviors work against each other, confusing us and leaving us feeling crazy rather than empowered. So make a decision. Will you continue to fight against yourself by dieting for weight loss while you entertain the idea of living in peace with your body? Or will you decide to trust your body wisdom about food, deeply embracing the notion that a peaceful relationship with your body, regardless of its size, is truly your heart's desire?

affirmation

Today I choose body-size acceptance over dieting

size-wise action

Can you remember a time in your life when you felt at peace? Go back, recapture the feeling. Imagine giving it to yourself right now, again, at this moment. Enjoy.

❧ Reflect beauty

Do you ever see large women in advertisements? Probably not. The media choose to represent all womanhood with young, thin females who are portrayed as popular, sexy, and successful. Since we don't see ourselves on TV, in magazines, or on billboards, it's hard to remember that we even exist, let alone that we can be popular, sexy, or successful. We do exist, so begin to notice large women—their beauty, their confidence, their successes. Admire them. Think of them as role models who can give you a confidence boost when you need one. Think of yourself as a role model of inner and outer beauty for other large women. Pretty soon, those thin young women in the media won't be the only ones who live the good life. You will be living it too!

affirmation

I am a reflection of inner and outer beauty.

size-wise action

Subscribe to the magazines *BBW* and *Radiance*. Having them delivered to your door can be a real boost to sagging spirits. You need look no further than the pages of these magazines to know that large women can be everything a thin woman can be—and more!

🌷 *The psychological stigma of fat is a lie*

The psychology of fat promotes the idea that there are emotional reasons for our weight. For example, we are repressing our anger and sexuality, we are emotionally overeating, or we are armoring ourselves with a "wall of fat." Although these psychological stereotypes have never been proved with research, they are believed just the same. How can we remove the psychological stigma from our body size and weight? One way is to live your life as a challenge to the notion that being fat *always* means being psychologically unhealthy. Transform the notion that fat is bad into an understanding that being fat is simply a variation in human size.

affirmation

I am free of the psychological stereotypes of fat.

size-wise action

Notice all the people you can today. Pay attention to the size of their bodies as well as their mood and behavior. Do *all* the fat people behave one way and *all* the thin people behave another? Are *all* the fat people angry and *all* the thin people pleasant? Record your observations in your journal.

❧ *Society has a weight problem*

Our culture promotes an ideal appearance for women that is almost impossible for anyone to attain. Even the models we see in the magazines wish they could look like their own images! It is important to realize that this "weight problem" does not belong to us personally. Our "wrong" weight is not a product of our own failing, our lack of will-power, or our being out of control. Our weight is "wrong" because our culture has decided it is wrong. But our bodies are not wrong! People have come in all sizes and shapes since the beginning of time. Just because society prefers a particular kind of body today is no reason to feel you have a weight problem. Remember this: You don't have a weight problem. Society does.

affirmation

My weight is perfect for me right now.

size-wise action

Empower yourself by becoming familiar with the history of feminine body image. Doing this will help you see that society's preferences in women's body type change because of economic and political factors, not because any particular body shape is better than all others.

❦ *Fat is not the centerpiece of your identity*

Psychologically speaking, our identities comprise many sides or parts of ourselves. A woman could identify herself as a gardener, lawyer, lover, grandmother, neighbor, volunteer, *and* a fat person. Such a woman sees her fat in a psychologically healthy way: as *one part* of her identity, not her *whole* identity. If we allow being fat to be the centerpiece of our identity, we may hamper ourselves in fully utilizing the other parts of ourselves. On the other hand, if we allow being fat to be part of us, we have more room to be and do everything else we can be and do. So take "fat" out of the center of your identity, and put it where it belongs—as a part of who you are, but not all of who you are.

affirmation

I am an expression of all the parts of myself.

size-wise action

Identify the various parts of yourself: the roles you play, the identities you have. Now reflect on how being fat plays into these parts of you. Are fat and the fat stereotype central to your view of yourself? Is fat in its rightful place as a part of you? Write about this in your journal.

❧ Inner-determining

Women who stop dieting and start accepting their bodies begin the process of living an inner-determining lifestyle. "Inner-determining" means making decisions about ourselves based on listening to our inner voice, rather than making decisions about ourselves based on listening to the collective voice of the culture. Because the culture's voice is strong, we have to keep reminding ourselves (sometimes on a moment-to-moment basis) to listen to our own inner voice and its wise messages of self-care. By listening to our inner voice we allow it to grow in strength and clarity until it drowns out the cultural messages. Determine the quality of your life by paying attention to your inner voice.

affirmation

I make decisions by listening to my inner voice.

size-wise action

Begin to develop your inner-determining lifestyle by doing two things: stop dieting, and start spending some quiet time with yourself. Practice listening carefully to your body's need for self-care.

Part 3

determination

❦ *Knowledge is power!*

It is very important to be knowledgeable about your weight, dieting, health, and body-image issues. This knowledge is obtained in two ways: first, by listening carefully to what your body has to say, and second, by reading the historical, medical, and research perspectives that verify your experience. Knowing these things can empower you when you are confronted by people (including your own critical voice) who think that accepting your body is a cop-out. Citing a research study or two that supports your experience raises your self-esteem. Why? Because you have asserted your right to your body and its truths. So read some research and listen carefully to your body. The combined knowledge is unbeatable!

affirmation

I am knowledgeable about my own body and health.

size-wise action

Read everything you can on weight-related issues that supports a nondieting, size-acceptance viewpoint. Memorize the details of one or two research studies and practice reciting their findings out loud—so that you'll be ready if confronted!

🌷 Assertiveness

Believe this: when people learn that you have begun the process of body-size acceptance, many of them will try to sabotage you in every way they can. The confrontations can come in many forms, from "I'm saying this for your own good," to "You're just rationalizing the fact that you don't have the discipline and self-control to lose weight." Prepare for these confrontations by developing your assertiveness. Assertiveness is a skill that can be learned, but you first have to believe that you deserve to stand up for yourself. You will feel deserving if you are knowledgeable about your body truths. So stick up for yourself, your body, your decisions, your life. It's your right.

affirmation

I am a strong and assertive woman.

size-wise action

Read a self-help book about assertiveness, or take an assertiveness training course at your local community college. It will be money and time well spent. After all, you deserve it!

❦ *Introspection is good for the soul*

While we are learning how to be more size-accepting, we need to build some quiet, reflective time into our lives. Quiet time allows us to center ourselves into our own truth and our own reality as women of size. Introspection allows us to consider our experiences as fat women and come to our own conclusions about our bodies and health. More important, introspection allows us to compare what *they* say about our bodies with what *we* experience and know about our body truths. Learn as much as you can from books. Listen to your body. Then look into yourself to see if you can capture the essence of who you are in the body you already have.

affirmation

I am wise because I am introspective about my life.

size-wise action

Schedule alone-time into your calendar. Mark it out with a big slash and write "MY TIME" in large letters. When your time comes up in your calendar, hang out with yourself in nurturing and creative ways: write in your journal, create something beautiful for yourself, or (fill in the blank). Reflect on your life as a woman of size.

Independent thinking opens doors to body acceptance

Thinking and behaving independently is very liberating. Just imagine a life determined by your own creative thinking and creative energy (rather than a life filled with trying to meet other people's expectations). A dream? It doesn't have to be. Your mind is capable of thinking anything you allow it to think. Just ask yourself whether you are *willing* to let go of other people's opinions in order to free your mind to go where you need it to go. If your answer is yes! then do it. Allow your mind to wander into the territory of what your life would be like if you accepted your body just as it is today. Think BOLD, BEAUTIFUL, COMFORTABLE, CONTENT! Think independently of the culture. Think for yourself.

affirmation
My mind is free to accept my body.

size-wise action
Activate the independent woman in you by considering this: what can I do today to be just a little bit outrageous (or very outrageous)? Do it and record your experience, including your feelings, in your journal.

✿ *Dieting costs big money*

How much money have you spent on dieting? How much money have you spent on enriching the quality of your life? If the dieting column adds up to more than the other column, it's time to realize that dieting not only drains your bank account, it also drains your resources for having those things that will actually enhance your life. Studies show that a chronic dieter spends $70,000 on diets in her lifetime, costing her an average of $1,000 a pound! Can you think of other ways to spend $70,000—ways that are more fun, enriching, and productive? The next time you take out your checkbook to pay for a diet product or service, remember that there are other ways to spend your money that will keep you feeling good. Invest in quality clothes, a vacation, a college course, a piece of art. Spend your money on something that lasts!

affirmation

I spend my money on things that enrich my life.

size-wise action

How much money have you spent on dieting? Make a decision to spend at least a small portion of that amount on something that makes you feel really, really good for a long, long time.

❦ *An open mind creates an open life*

Being classified as different creates personal shame and public discrimination. Fat people are seen as different, in the out-group, off in left field. We know what it's like to be chosen last, if we're chosen at all. Yet look around. There are others who are out in left field with us: minorities, the poor, the aged, the homeless, battered women, and others. It is fitting that we fat women develop empathy and sensitivity for others who, like us, are watching from the sidelines. Developing open-mindedness toward other groups that are discriminated against gives us support for our place in this society: none of us are *bad*. We're just *different*. And being different is nothing to be ashamed of.

affirmation

I am accepting of "differentness" in myself and others.

size-wise action

Think about other groups who are discriminated against by society and see if you can find a way to reach out in thought or action. Send money to a food pantry, volunteer at a battered women's shelter, or visit an elderly couple on your street. Remind yourself of your connection to other out-groups.

❦ Get out of the "fat mentality" and into your life

People with a "fat mentality" buy into the fat stereotypes: "I can't do this because I'm fat." Building size-esteem, on the other hand, depends on this: "I can do this because I want to." Notice the absence of weight as an indicator of ability to do or not do something. Weight can be used as an excuse for anything a person does not want to do. The problem with this approach to life is that the person with a fat mentality winds up not having much of a life. So if you use your weight as an excuse to not have a life, get *off* it! You can choose to have a life in the body you already have. Get out of the fat mentality and into your life.

affirmation

I am willing to live the life I want and deserve.

size-wise action

The next time you think, "I can't, because I'm too fat," stop and think of the real reason you "can't." Fear? Shame? Embarrassment? What? Examine the emotion. Get to the root of it. Then change your mind about what you can and cannot do in the body you already have.

❦ *Live for today*

Do you realize that this moment, the moment you are reading these words, is the only moment you have? You can't live in the past because the past exists only in your memory, and you can't live in the future because the future exists only in your imagination. *This* moment is the only one you have, so live it with full awareness—even if you are fat! Don't put off living today because you aren't thin enough. If you hear yourself say, "When I lose weight I will...," STOP. Remind yourself that life is passing you by. Get on with it. Get on with your life regardless of your weight. *Tempus fugit.* Tick-tock.

affirmation

Today I choose to live every moment to its fullest.

size-wise action

What do you want to do with your life that isn't based on your appearance? What do you want to experience while you still can? Write these things in your journal, and use your list as a reminder (especially when you're tempted to go on another diet) of what your life is really about, before your time runs out.

❧ Get on with it

If you live your whole life with an emphasis on losing weight, you'll wind up losing your life instead! Diets come and go. Weight comes off and goes on, off and on. Up and down, off and on. It's like a merry-go-round, only we aren't so "merry" when we are riding ourselves about our weight. So get off your weight and get on with your life. Accumulate evidence that you can have a full life in your full body. Choose to do something meaningful with your time, something that will last longer than the "success" you experienced on your last diet, something you can feel great about *this* year and *all* the years of your life.

affirmation

I am living a full and meaningful life.

size-wise action

Raise your self-esteem by choosing only meaningful and self-caring projects. Make a list of what they are. Keep track of the things you do every day that give real meaning to your life. Remind yourself that there is more to your life than losing weight.

 *Competence*

A major step in building size-esteem is to focus on those things we can do well and then do them with gusto. Recognizing our competence is important, because we have been encouraged to feel successful primarily in the dieting arena. Since only 5 percent of the dieting population wins the weight-loss game, where does that leave the rest of us? Can we *all* be failures? No! Dieting is a setup for failure, whereas doing those things in which we are competent is a setup for success. Know yourself as a competent woman even if you don't have the perfect body. Begin by putting your achievements at the top of the list of who you are.

affirmation

I am competent in all that I do.

size-wise action

List the things in which you are competent. These things do not have to be indicators of fame; they can be your big and small successes every day. Think about the ways you have been challenged and have met those challenges. All of these are clues to where your competence lies. Update your list and read it often. There's more to being a success than losing weight!

 *Courage*

Living as a nondieting, size-accepting woman takes a full measure of courage, because the culture insists that dieting is the only appropriate behavior for us. So when we say No! to dieting and Yes! to our lives, we are taking bold, brave, daring, undaunted, fearless, rebellious, unshrinking, stouthearted, indomitable, persevering, and courageous steps in living our lives. Isn't that better than living in fear and shame? You bet it is! Give shame back to the culture, and take back your life as a woman of size—courageously!

affirmation

I am a brave and courageous woman.

size-wise action

Develop the quality of mind and spirit that enables you to face size discrimination with self-determination and courage. Begin by recognizing that you have a right to the life you desire in the body you already have. Ask yourself what your life would be like if you dumped shame and boldly took back your life. Write about this life in your journal.

 *Confidence*

Do you know women who just seem to breathe confidence? Whatever they do, whatever they say, they do it and say it with assurance, grace, and certainty. Well, that woman can be you! When you make the courageous decision to have a life in the body you already have, this "I'm good!" attitude spills over into the rest of your life as confidence. Confidence is a way of believing in yourself, in what you do. Confidence is about trusting your wisdom. As you gather evidence that you have made wise decisions, your confidence builds. Confidence comes from a belief that you're worth something. In fact, you're worth *everything*.

affirmation

I exude confidence in everything I do.

size-wise action

Find someone who exudes confidence and ask her to lunch. Tell her you admire her confidence. Ask her to share with you some of her secrets for building confidence. Write these secrets down and practice them as often as possible.

❦ *Empowerment*

Empowerment is an enticing word because it implies po-
tency, energy, control, and strength. Many people
want to feel empowered, but few people can handle what it
means: relying on an internal rather than external authority.
Women of size have a hard time developing an internal sense
of authority because the external pressure to conform our
bodies to the cultural ideal is enormous. How then do larger
women become empowered? By getting completely in touch
with our largeness, our largesse in body and gifts. Only then
will we know that our power in the world is not diminished
by our size, but *enhanced* by it. The truth of the matter is,
we're worth our weight in gold!

affirmation

I am empowered by my size.

size-wise action

Write about your ideal life, your ultimate fantasy. Put
in all the rich details that come to mind. Now pick
out some ways in which you can begin to make your
real life look like your fantasy life *without changing
your body*. Take control. Empower yourself from the
inside out.

✿ *Health and weight are unrelated*

People have health problems regardless of their weight. Having a body—fat or thin—means having things go wrong with it, whether it's a common cold or cancer. So if you do have a health concern, try to separate it from your concerns about your size even if it's a disease that has been related to "obesity." Feeling guilty about being fat will not cure you of your health problems. In fact, feeling guilty will lead you to unhealthy behaviors, such as isolating yourself or being unable to make an appointment with a doctor to find out what is really wrong. Feeling guilty about your health and weight gets in the way of your being healthy. Blaming all your health problems on your weight is not the answer.

affirmation

I separate my health issues from my weight.

size-wise action

When you have a health concern, see your physician! Assert your right to appropriate health care by discussing your views about your health and weight. Either educate your doctor to be size-friendly or find another health-care provider who is.

❦ *Largeness does not equal unhappiness*

You might look in the mirror and see yourself and your size as something you wish were different. You might even say you dislike the reflection you see, that you are dissatisfied with the way you look. These judgments about your appearance, however, do not have to affect the totality and quality of your life. You can still feel good about yourself in the body you already have. Part of this "feeling good" process involves focusing *more* on the other things in your life that are important to you, and focusing *less* on the importance of your size. I mean, you might also wish you were smarter or richer, but that doesn't stop you from living, does it?

affirmation

I am a large and happy woman.

size-wise action

What can you change to make your life happier? If you can't significantly change your size, your intelligence, or your bank account, what can you change? Focus on those things and put your energy there. What can you do today to make your life a little bit happier?

❦ *Expand your definition of beauty*

There is more to beauty than the images that show up in the pages of *Vogue* and *Glamour*—a lot more! Beauty is a matter of individual perception, as in "Beauty is in the eye of the beholder." Our aesthetic can be trained to appreciate beauty beyond the narrow range that is pushed on us by fashion magazines, TV, and billboards. Remember, it wasn't so long ago that African American beauty was unappreciated in our culture. Because African Americans in the 1960s and '70s made a conscious effort to reclaim their culture and their definition of beauty, our cultural definition of what is beautiful has broadened to include "Black is beautiful!" The same can be done for women of size. Reclaim your right to be a big *and* beautiful woman.

affirmation

I am a big, beautiful woman.

size-wise action

When you notice a big, beautiful woman, compliment her on her appearance. Hold her in your memory as a mirror to your own beauty. Begin to train your aesthetics to include images of big women as beautiful. Add yourself to the big-and-beautiful category of women.

❦ *The fat stereotypes are a lie*

A re you a fat woman who fits the fat stereotypes? Probably not. It's the *culture's attitude* toward fat people that perpetuates these stereotypes. They have nothing to do with your life or the lives of other large women you know. Look around. How many large women do you see sitting around eating bonbons? Most large women are leading full, creative, busy lives as lawyers, teachers, artists, secretaries, cooks, writers, wives, mothers, grandmothers, and lovers. Free yourself from the shadow of the fat stereotypes. Do not accept as your own culture's interpretation of your body type. If the culture says, "You can't do that because you're fat," you say, "Watch me!" Then do it.

affirmation

I appreciate my uniqueness as a larger woman.

size-wise action

Find one thing you can do today to consciously defy the fat stereotypes. You might refuse to participate in diet talk; wear shorts in public; openly admire another large woman for her talents, ideas, or appearance. Think of other ways in which you can defy the fat stereotypes.

🌷 *Change your mind to fit your body*

How many years have you been dieting? How many years have you tried to change your body to fit some image that doesn't even come close to who you are? How much longer will you try to change your body to fit your mind? Well, you don't have to think about your body in the same way anymore! You have the power to change your mind to fit your body—the same body you're living in today. Just think: no more diets, no more hating your reflection, no more shame and guilt, no more depriving yourself of clothing, fun, relationships, or happiness. It's simple. Just change your mind about your body.

affirmation

I think about my body in respectful and loving ways.

size-wise action

Pretend that this is the last week you are going to be alive. Think about all the things you've always wanted to do. What would you like to accomplish in the time you have left? Is losing weight at the top of your list? Your body, thin or fat, will eventually die, whereas you accomplishments will live on. Accomplish something important today.

Body-size acceptance is a process

Accepting our bodies, in their variety of shapes and sizes, is a difficult task for women in this culture. Someone or something is always reminding us that our bodies do not measure up. We must resist giving in to the cultural message that we are unacceptable and begin the process of accepting our bodies just as they are. Accepting our bodies is not something that happens overnight just because we wish it to be so. The first step in this process is to say that you are *willing* to accept your body exactly as it is today. Then consciously choose people, situations, and actions that support this decision.

affirmation

I accept my body the way it is right now.

size-wise action

If you are still dieting, or thinking about going on a diet, please consider this: dieting is an attempt to change your body, not to accept it as it is. Try going through today without dieting or thinking about dieting. Write about this experience in your journal.

 *Balance*

Remember when you were a girl, playing on a teeter-totter? At first it was fun just to go up and down, but when that got boring, you took on the challenge of trying to balance yourself. Living as a larger women is much like being on that teeter-totter: sometimes you're feeling up (weight loss), and then something brings you down again (weight gain). Up and down, endlessly. Wouldn't it be wonderful to have your physical, emotional, intellectual, and spiritual life be in balance regardless of your weight? It can be done! The trick is to focus on *all* the parts of yourself and not let your weight command your total time and attention. There is much more to you than your body weight.

affirmation

I am balanced in body, mind, emotions, and spirit.

size-wise action

Draw a circle on a piece of paper. Divide the circle into four sections, each proportional to the amount of time you spend on your body, mind, emotions, and spirit. Look at their proportions. Are they balanced? Where could you put more of your attention? Make a list of what you can do to balance your time among all the parts of yourself.

❦ *Our culture's current preference for thinness is arbitrary*

If you look at the preferred body types for women over the centuries, you will notice that the culture's preferences change periodically. Eras of fashionable fatness are followed by years of fashionable thinness. The important thing to remember is that these preferences are *arbitrary*; that is, they have been determined by the whims of fashion designers and by the economics of the health and insurance industries. They have nothing to do with your value in the world. There have always been fat women, thin women, and in-between women. The culture's preference for a certain size and shape of our bodies is not related to the real quality of our lives.

affirmation

All women's bodies, including my own, are beautiful.

size-wise action

Go to the library and find the art of Rubens, Renoir, and Botero. Begin to appreciate the beauty of the larger bodies they painted. Translate your appreciation of those women's beauty into appreciation of your own beauty.

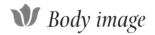 *Body image*

Body image is an internal experience: our experience of our body on a visual (seeing) level, an auditory (hearing) level, and a kinesthetic (moving) level. Your personal body image is a combination of the body you see when you close your eyes, what you say to yourself about your body, and how you feel inside your body while moving. Body image is also an external experience: how the culture sees the kind of body you have. The cultural body image will affect your personal body image by influencing the way you see your body, talk to your body, and move your body. Be aware of your body image. Is it a true reflection of who you are in your body? Or has it been distorted by the culture, with its emphasis on thinness?

affirmation

I am comfortable with my body.

size-wise action

Read *Bodylove* by Rita Freedman. Practice the exercises. They were designed to shift your body image from negative and rejecting to positive and accepting.

🌱 *Body image is fluid and changeable*

Body image is a slippery thing. One moment we like the way we look and the next moment we don't. In many ways, body image is dependent on how we feel about our *behavior* toward our body. If you've just finished an exhilarating walk and feel energized and strong, your body image tends to be positive. If you go out to dinner and eat so much that you feel bloated and weak, however, your body image will probably take a turn toward the negative. Bad or good, thin or fat—body image changes along with the internal experience of your behavior. Accept your body image as fluid and changeable, because it is.

affirmation

I accept my changing body image.

size-wise action

If you're having a negative body-image moment, try this: do something positive. For example, take a walk, get a massage, eat if you're hungry and stop when you're full. Learn that you can change your negative body image into a positive one.

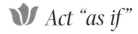 *Act "as if"*

Acting "as if" involves behaving in practice as we would want to behave if we possessed all our desired qualities. This is a useful tool for larger women because we have spent much of our lives waiting to be thin people, who are, of course, the only people allowed to have perfect lives! They aren't. We can have our perfect lives too. Acting "as if" allows us to practice the behavior we think is only for thin people. By acting "as if," we learn that we don't have to wait until we are thin to have the life we want.

affirmation

I act as if I have a right to my life in the body I already have.

size-wise action

Think about something you want to do but have been putting off doing until you lose weight. Act "as if" you can do it right now. Go ahead. Give yourself permission to practice this behavior. Watch what happens in your life. Record in your journal the consequences of acting "as if."

❦ Create your body image

When you look in the mirror, what do you see? If you see yourself reflected back as *smaller*, you have a creative body image. When we larger women underestimate our size, we are not in denial, or crazy, or anything like that. We are actually responding to a sick culture in a psychologically healthy way: seeing ourselves as smaller allows us to act as if we are a smaller size, which in turn allows us to move through life less encumbered by fat stereotypes. We can act as if our size is not an issue. Having a creative body image is really a tool for living a quality life in the bodies we already have.

affirmation

I am creative in my thoughts about my body.

size-wise action

Minimize the effects of the fat stereotypes in your life by re-creating your body image. Begin by accepting your smaller (creative) body image into your life as a healthy reaction to a sick culture. Write about your creative body image in your journal.

❧ Transfigured body image

Not all of us have a creative body image—that is, not all of us see ourselves as smaller. Some large women look at themselves in the mirror or photographs and say, "Yes, this is me!" without flinching, judging, being shocked, or fainting. They see themselves just as big as the camera or mirror reflects back to them. These women have a transfigured body image. This means that they have transformed their perceptions of their bodies by adopting a matter-of-fact view of themselves as fat. They don't judge fat as bad. Their body image and their judgments about body size have moved away from "bad" to "this is me." Period. Having a transfigured body image is a comfortable place to be.

affirmation
I see a reflection of myself in my body size.

size-wise action
If you see yourself as smaller, don't worry about developing a transfigured body image. Just keep living your life in the body you already have, and eventually you'll come to a place of both seeing and accepting yourself just as you are.

 Satisfaction

There are many studies on the relationship between women's body image and their degree of depression or satisfaction with their lives. One study found that the label a woman assigns to her weight will affect her self-esteem. Another reports that women who are depressed distort their body image in a negative direction (I am a big, fat slob), while nondepressed women distort their body image in an enhancing way (I am a big, beautiful woman). Putting these findings together, it makes sense that larger women who posses a creative or transfigured body image will tend to be less depressed about their body size and more satisfied with their lives than will larger women who still think of their bodies as unacceptable. So create the body image that works for you, and feel yourself becoming more satisfied.

affirmation

I am satisfied with my body exactly as it is today.

size-wise action

Begin to associate the word *big* with positive thoughts such as "making it big" and "big-hearted." Then translate "big" into a positive description of who you are.

❦ A distorted body image comes from a distorted culture

Some psychotherapists talk about larger women with "distorted" body images—body images that don't match the "reality" of their bodies. We need to ask ourselves a different question about this: are women's body images distorted, or is it our cultural belief about fat that is distorted? According to today's myths, a woman can't do certain things if she is fat: she can't be brilliant, creative, beautiful. In fact, she's not supposed to have a life at all! But this is not the experience of many large women. We know that the current stereotypes about fat people don't apply to us, because we are busy leading full, productive lives. So where is the distortion? It lives in the larger culture, not in the lives of larger women!

affirmation

I see myself and my body as acceptable.

size-wise action

Think about the fat stereotypes. How many of them fit you? If you are living out the cultural distortion of what a fat woman should be, STOP! Start living like the woman you were born to be.

 *Shame*

Body shame is a big issue in the lives of most women. This is because our bodies are valued primarily for their appearance. Since the culture has a strict definition of physical beauty, and since most women's bodies do not conform to this definition, most women feel that they aren't thin enough or "attractive" enough. This creates body shame. Shame is a feeling that you are a bad person, rather than feeling that you have done a bad thing (which is guilt). Shame is about secrecy and isolation. Body shame is the worst kind of shame because it shakes us in the very core of our humanness. Body shame is something that women must reject and give back to the culture. Remember this: you never, ever have done anything in your life bad enough to merit the shame the culture puts on you for having a woman's body.

affirmation

I am a beautiful, worthwhile woman.

size-wise action

Practice saying, "You can't shame me anymore!" Say this especially when you see the "perfect" woman's body on TV, in magazines, or on billboards. Dump shame. Reclaim your body.

❦ *Let your spirit lead your body*

Women of all shapes and sizes need to recognize that our bodies are important and that it makes sense to take care of them. But women also need to acknowledge that we have valuable intellectual, emotional, and creative lives. When we balance all the facets of ourselves that we use for expression in the world, we reach a point where we allow our spiritual nature to give us direction. When spirit leads body, mind, and emotions, we become more centered in the reality of who we actually are, and our everyday decisions and behaviors become more grounded in that reality. When we allow our spirit to lead the rest of us, we find we have a more fulfilling and meaningful life, regardless of body size.

affirmation

I allow my spiritual energy to direct my life.

size-wise action

Imagine what your spiritual nature looks like, feels like, sounds like, even tastes like! Now imagine this is "you" being expressed in little ways every day. What would today look like with your spirit leading your body?

 *Surrender*

When we think of surrendering, we often think of giving up, losing a fight, being defeated. But *surrendering* has another meaning: letting go, moving on. When it comes to their bodies, most people believe they have to be diligent about food and exercise, exerting willpower and self-control so that they don't lose the battle of the bulge. This kind of attitude and behavior goes against nature, because sometimes it's not possible to be in control of our bodies. Sometimes our bodies have minds of their own. Sometimes we have to surrender to the truth of the body: it is what it is. Surrendering to being a larger woman is not giving up, or being defeated, or even losing a battle. It is letting go. Let go, and positively surrender to your body's truths.

affirmation

I surrender to the truth of my body.

size-wise action

Don't the words *let go* and *surrender* make you want to breathe easier? So breathe in and think "surrender"; then breathe out and think "let go." In and out. Surrender to the truth about your body. Let go into your life.

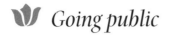 *Going public*

Women who become involved in the process of size acceptance often become more comfortable in allowing themselves to be exactly who they are—in public! This means that they are able to speak or behave freely, without shame about their body size. When they do, they send a powerful message to everyone who is watching: You can't shame me anymore! I am a fat woman who is free to be whoever I want. Some examples of going public are letting people know you don't appreciate fat jokes; ordering dessert in a restaurant; refusing to talk about diets; asking for a bigger chair; wearing shorts in public; owning a bathing suit. Take pride in yourself. Go out into the world and show everyone who you *really* are, publicly!

affirmation

I publicly affirm my value and worth as a woman of size.

size-wise action

Pick one of the "going public" actions listed above (or any other action that you can think of) and make a commitment to carry it out today.

 *Role model*

In the later stages of size acceptance, women often find themselves in the interesting position of becoming role models for other women. Being a role model sounds like a big responsibility. After all, it implies that others are looking up to you as a guide, someone they can emulate. But becoming a role model really happens quietly—to women who go about their lives fully. When any woman does that, especially a larger woman, the world takes notice: "Gee, she's fat *and* she has a life? Amazing!" So if someone notices you, looks to you for direction and inspiration, don't be scared or think that you have to do anything more than you're doing right now. Just be yourself and feel good that other women are learning by your example.

affirmation

I live my life in a way that sets a positive example for other large women.

size-wise action

Find a larger woman to admire, respect, and emulate. Watch her tactics, her behavior, her attitude. Practice making those attributes your own.

🌷 *Some things are larger than we are*

Sometimes it's hard to remember that there is more to the world and more to ourselves than having a large body. Living in a larger body can be mind-consuming as well as time-consuming. For some of us, our body has become an obsession, pervading every thought and action. For others, being large is like a shadow following us around, never letting us forget that no matter what else we do, we are fat. Yet we are more than our bodies. This is a very basic and important realization, one we should never forget. So connect to something larger that yourself, and be thankful that you have a vehicle, your body, for expressing yourself in the world.

affirmation

I am connected to something larger than myself.

size-wise action

Try to connect to those things in your life that are beyond body obsession. Think of the times when you have given something back to the world through your actions. Think about the larger you, the one that resides in your spirit, not your body. Write about this in your journal.

♥ *Leadership*

Becoming a size-accepting woman sometimes means inspiring other large women to do the same. Once you experience freedom from body obsession, it's exciting to share your victory with others. Leadership for size acceptance might involve taking an active role in NAAFA, giving public testimony about how your life has changed since you've accepted your body, writing articles or leading workshops on size acceptance, or helping to organize a fitness program for large women. What's important about this? Everything! These actions (and others) transform the original stigma of being fat into something meaningful and worthwhile—for you, other women, *and* the culture.

affirmation

I show leadership as a larger woman by making contributions to my community.

size-wise action

Just as the flutter of a butterfly's wings can change the weather a thousand miles away, every public action, no matter how small, can change the world's view of larger women. Do something today that will lead others toward fuller acceptance of their larger lives.

❦ A roomy life

Dieting and body-hate sap women's energy, giving us a narcissistic obsession with having the perfect body. In fact, this energy depletion is so great that a woman who is preoccupied with her body barely has room for anything else in her life: personal accomplishments often take second place to her ultimate goal of having the perfect body or are tainted by a pervasive feeling of never being "good enough." Nondieting, size-accepting women, on the other hand, have a roomy life. Since body concerns are balanced with other parts of their lives, these women have more time to live their dreams. This is a spacious, "good enough" place to be!

affirmation

I make room in my life for the important things I want to accomplish.

size-wise action

Imagine a large, empty room. This room represents the time you have to do all the things you want to do. Now imagine filling up that room with your personal accomplishments, one by one. See what a beautiful room (life) you can create for yourself!

❦ *Give support!*

In the later phases of learning to accept our bodies, we find that support itself goes through a transition: instead of focusing completely on *getting* support, we begin *giving* support to others. Providing support to others may or may not be intentional. It happens primarily because a size-accepting woman is a role model for others who are beginning the process of size acceptance. Remember, any large woman who *has a life* will be noticed, since she is defying the stereotypes about fat people. Other large women need to see a reflection of who they can be, so when you become a source of support to them, you really help them move along with their process. Support is a gift that keeps on giving!

affirmation

I support others who are building size-esteem.

size-wise action

If you are a woman who is comfortable with her size, please remember this: when you are in the company of women, what you do and how you express yourself supports other large women. Give yourself and other women support whenever, however, you can.

❧ *There is more to you than your body*

Human beings exist on several planes: physical, emotional, intellectual, and spiritual. All these are vehicles for expressing our personality in the world. However, we are more than our body, more than our mind, more than our emotions. And our spiritual nature encompasses them all. It is a good practice to become fully aware of *all* that expresses who we are. That way, if you spend too much time in one realm (body), you'll remember to spend some time in the others. Women who spend a majority of their time in the body realm rarely have any energy left over for using their intellect, for expressing the variety of emotions that come with being human, or for exploring their spiritual nature by using their intuition and creativity. You have a body, and you are more than your body!

affirmation

I am more than my body.

size-wise action

Say the affirmation, "I am more than my body" every time you become obsessed with negative body-thoughts.

❧ *Express the "more" of you*

Remembering that we are more than our body takes constant vigilance. After all, the culture (in all its many forms) constantly reminds women that *all* we are is a body— a body to be changed, shaped, exercised, dieted, liposuctioned, implanted, deodorized, shaved, made-up, dressed up, and more. No wonder we find it difficult to move out of body self-consciousness into a conscious and spirited self! One way to stay aware of all your parts is to find ways to connect with your self, your "spirit," in affirming and self-loving ways. Watch how your spirit encourages you to go beyond the bounds of your body and into your life as a multifaceted woman. Then express the "more" of you, magically transforming your life into something larger than yourself.

affirmation

I express who I am with everything I do.

size-wise action

Express the "more" of you by finding ways to exercise your creative muscle or by exploring ways to give something back to your community.

🌷 *Learn to see the world through your size, not in spite of it*

Life in a larger body is filled with all kinds of hurt, anxiety, and pain—from worry over airplane seating to dealing with people who want to "save" you from being fat by making comments about what you're eating. Let's face it, life's no picnic if you're bigger than a size eight. It's no wonder that fat people think the answer to their problems is to go on another diet. But that has been the wrong answer for decades, so we must find other ways to live large, and with dignity! One way is to change how you view yourself and the world. Instead of saying, "I'm fat and I have to become thin," say, "I'm fat. So?" Learn to see the world and your body as abundant. Be at peace with both.

affirmation

I view the world as an abundant source of peace and happiness.

size-wise action

Make a list of all the abundance in your life, the good things, the joys. Remind yourself that you have created these things in the body you already have.

 *Become a rebel!*

There is something exciting and energizing about being called a rebel. Rebellion has always been the most dramatic way to make sweeping changes; it has fueled everything from the formation of new countries to the creation of unique art movements. Being a rebel requires energy and commitment, the kind that will move the old way out and the new way in. Finally, rebels need a worthy cause to fight for. What better cause do women have than to "fight the good fight" about weight and size discrimination. Fighting for the right to live our lives in the bodies we already have is essential for us to move on, to get beyond body-size obsession. So become a rebel! Accept yourself as you are right now, and encourage other women to do the same.

affirmation

I act on my life the way I see fit.

size-wise action

When was the last time you rebelled? Whenever it was, it was too long ago! Think about how you can rebel against society's dictates of thinness, and then do it!

❦ *Healthful eating is not the same as dieting*

Making healthy choices about our bodies is tough. On one side the "experts" preach to us about the sins of food and the evils of eating, while on the other the advertisers bombard us with food images everywhere we look, begging us to eat hamburgers, candy, pizzas, everything the "food police" say will kill us. How do we get out of this trap of food seduction and guilt? By choosing health over dieting. By choosing to become attuned to the body's wisdom: what it needs for nourishment balanced by what it wants for pleasure. By choosing to see yourself as a healthy large woman who neither gives in to the seduction of eating what she doesn't want nor feels guilty about food.

affirmation
I choose healthful eating over dieting.

size-wise action
Learn to differentiate between foods that call out to you from the ads and foods that hum from your body wisdom. Choose to eat what hums as often as possible. And stop dieting!

❦ *Accepting your body takes time*

The process of moving from body-hate to body acceptance cannot be hurried. It takes time, because, even though we desire to be at peace with our bodies, we are also scared. The cultural conditioning regarding our bodies is so complete, we are afraid that letting go of body-hate will leave a big void in us—a space so big and wide that we'll never be able to fill it. When something so deeply ingrained is being taken away, something else has to take its place. Be patient with yourself while you are finding ways to replace negative body-thinking, thought by thought, with positive body-thinking. Each day, indeed each *moment*, that you can free yourself from negative and obsessive thinking about your body is a gift to yourself. Take it one moment at a time.

affirmation

I am grateful for every day I live peacefully in my body.

size-wise action

Meditate on the word *patience*. Imagine yourself moving toward body acceptance like a leaf on a slow-moving stream. Enjoy the ride.

🌷 *You are the expert on your life*

Experts are a dime a dozen. Everyone with an opinion (and that's everyone on the planet) feels an urge at one time or another to tell others what to do, believe, think, or feel, how to run their lives. Look around. Advice from "experts" is everywhere. Uncritical acceptance of other people's opinions and advice on how to solve our problems is very dangerous, because it depletes our confidence in our own decision-making ability. So follow your own expertise—the kind that comes from trusting your experience and listening to your inner voice. You don't need another expert to tell you how to live your life in the body you already have. *You are the expert.*

affirmation

I have all the expertise I need to make good decisions about my body and my life.

size-wise action

The next time you have to decide something, especially related to your body, STOP. Remember that you know everything you need to know to make this decision.

🌷 *Spirituality*

Accepting your body as it is, without judgment, is one way of expressing your spirituality. Ask yourself this: does my body *size* have anything to do with how spiritual I am? Probably, it does not. Yet certain body-related behaviors do affect your spirituality on a day-to-day basis—for example, how you respect, care for, and love your body; how you view your body as part of nature's plan of beauty and diversity; how you wisely use your body as your vehicle for doing good works in the world. Begin to understand deeply that you have a spiritual life connected to your body, yet bigger than your body.

affirmation

I value my body as a way of expressing my spirituality.

size-wise action

Make the connection between your physical life as a larger woman and your spiritual life. Do you let your body or your spirit speak the truth of who you are? Think of one way in which you can let your spirit have a voice in what you do today. Then do it.

❦ *Body-size acceptance is a spiraling process rather than a linear process*

Our rational, linear-thinking society tells us that if we want to get to C, we must do A and B. It's hard for us even to think about a problem without concluding that there is only one way to solve it. But the process of body-size acceptance defies such a formulaic description. Size acceptance does not move in the straight line of first you do this, then you do that, and then you're finished. It is much more complex. So instead of thinking about the process of accepting your body as a straight line from A to B to C, think of it as a spiral-like staircase that weaves around itself as it moves up or down. The point is this: your process will be as individual as you are.

affirmation

I move through the process of size acceptance at my own pace, rhythm, and speed.

size-wise action

Map out your process of body-size acceptance. Draw it with all the rich detail you can. Mark important places, decisions, and behaviors. Keep adding to it as a way of understanding your process.

❦ *Don't apologize!*

An apology is appropriate when we have done something we regret or when we want to ask pardon for a fault or offense. An apology is not appropriate when it comes to talking about your body. Never, under any circumstances, apologize for your size! Your body size is nothing to be ashamed of. You are not bad, nor do you deserve to feel guilty because you weigh more than the culture says a woman ought to weigh. Save your apologies for things you've done wrong. Your body is not one of those things. Your body is not wrong. Respect your body even if the culture doesn't. Respect yourself.

affirmation

I have a right to live my life proudly as a larger woman.

size-wise action

Listen to yourself on two levels—what you say to others and what you say to yourself inside your head. Notice how many times you want to apologize, to say you're sorry for being a large woman. Monitor your statements so they do not include "I'm sorry" when it comes to talking about your body size.

 *Space*

Do you find yourself shrinking, holding in, squeezing, sucking in, slouching, compressing, or tightening your body to fit within a certain space? That space could be an airplane aisle or seat, a booth at a restaurant, a chair with arms, a turnstile, a movie theater seat, or a desk in a classroom. Space is a problem for larger people because most public places have been designed to accommodate only the size eights of the world. Movie theaters, restaurants, schools, and airlines must not know that over thirty million women in this country wear a size sixteen or larger. Quit squeezing and slouching. Take a stand and take up your space. You have a right to be accommodated in public places.

affirmation

I am entitled to take up as much space as I need.

size-wise action

Ask for a bigger chair, or an armless chair, without shame. Write to the airlines and theaters, letting them know that their seats are designed for children, not most adults. Spend your money in places that accommodate your size, and let them know you appreciate their efforts to welcome you and your money.

🌱 *A healthy mind does not equal a skinny body*

Some people would have you believe that if you really had it together mentally and emotionally, you'd be thin. This is a lie. Those people are promoting the "healthy mind, skinny body" philosophy that excludes millions of larger men and women. In fact, this philosophy exists to make everyone but the skinniest people feel ashamed of themselves and guilty about not doing enough to be "healthy" (i.e., thin). While claiming to lead us toward health and wholeness, this philosophy is in fact a trap to keep us compulsively working to become thin. Your larger body is not an indication of an unhealthy mind or sick emotions. Healthy emotions come in all sizes. Healthy minds come in all sizes. And healthy bodies come in all sizes.

affirmation

I have a healthy mind and body.

size-wise action

Do a study of all the people you know. Which of those people have the healthiest emotions? The healthiest minds? What kinds of bodies do they have? Make the connection: the size of a person's body is unrelated to the health of her or his emotions and intellect. Write about this in your journal.

❦ Beware of diets in disguise

In the last couple of years, diet programs have gotten a bad name. In part, this is because some of the programs have seemed more interested in their profits than in the good health of their clients. The truth about diets is also being exposed by those of us who have been on them most of our lives: diets don't work on a permanent basis. They never have, they never will. But there is a lot of money in dieting—billions of dollars that the dieting industry is unwilling to lose. Its answer? Diets in disguise! These programs use clever phrases such as "lifestyle changes" or "the no-diet diet" or "diets don't work but ours does." You've seen the advertisements. These programs are seductive—and they are still ineffective! So become a detective. If it costs you money, if it promises weight loss, it is still a diet, no matter what it's called.

affirmation

I eat in a healthful and inner-directed way.

size-wise action

Break your addiction to dieting. Learn how to eat in a natural, normal, healthful way. Check the back pages of *Live Large!* for resources that can help you take this step.

❦ Transformation

Transformation is a very big deal! It means taking something (an idea, action, behavior, or philosophy) and converting it, markedly changing it, into something else. There is a certain magic associated with transformation, a certain mystique surrounding those who have transformed themselves. Just think of our movie idols and you'll get the picture. Well, film stars aren't the only ones who can do this. You can too! You can transform your thinking about your body: from "fat and ugly" to "big and beautiful"; from "fat and worthless" to "large and in charge"; from "fat and frumpy" to "abundant and radiant." Get the idea? Change the way you think about yourself, and watch yourself magically transform before your very eyes.

affirmation

I choose to transform the nature of my body-thoughts.

size-wise action

Whenever your old negative thinking comes up, practice saying "big and beautiful," "large and in charge," or "abundant and radiant." Remind yourself that you are a *transformer* of your thoughts from negative to positive.

❧ *Be who you want to be*

When someone is categorized into a stereotype (any stereotype), the rest of the world has a set view of how that person should be, regardless of how that person really is. When someone is larger than the cultural ideal, the rest of the world expects her to "act like a fat person." What is a fat person supposed to act like, anyway? Lazy? Stupid? Slovenly? Is that you? Is that anyone else you know who is fat? Probably not. Don't you know skinny people who are lazy or stupid or slovenly? Probably. Size and personality are unrelated. Size and grooming are unrelated. So don't buy into how you're supposed to be as a fat woman. Be who you are, regardless of your size.

affirmation

I am the woman I really want to be.

size-wise action

What do you want to be? Who are you, *really*? Write about these things in your journal. Bring your words out often to remind yourself that you are not the fat stereotype. You are YOU!

🌷 *Don't wait to get thin to get what you want out of life*

Are you waiting to get thin to get what you want? You might as well try to get home by waiting for a bus in the middle of the Sahara. In other words, thinness is not the vehicle for getting you anywhere, let alone where you need and want to be. Thinness is the size of a body, not the size of your life. Thinness comes naturally to only a few, and chances are (especially if you've spent your life dieting), you may not be one of those people. So forget about getting thin and remember to get a life-the life you want-in the body you already have.

affirmation

Today I choose to have one thing I really want, regardless of my size.

size-wise action

Look at your thin friends. Do they have perfect lives? Do they never get sick, never fight with their partners, never get turned down for a job, never have to pay bills? Remind yourself that the perfect life comes with the willingness to have it. Get willing.

🌷 *Decide what your size means to you*

Build size-esteem by becoming decisive about what your size means to you. In doing this, you are rejecting society's interpretation of your body size and accepting your own interpretation instead. That's an empowering place to be! It means you are in control of your thinking about your body, your decisions about your body, your behavior regarding your body, and your feelings towards your body. That is how it should be, because *it is your body!* So take back the power to determine what your body size means to you. Be okay in your body. Take care of your body. Have a full and rewarding life in your body. Feel proud of yourself in your body.

affirmation

I empower myself to determine the meaning of my size.

size-wise action

Build self-esteem by making decisions about your life in the present moment. Then act on them. What is one thing you can do today to feel proud of who you are? Now go do it.

🌷 *Food can be a nonissue in your life*

For women who have spent years (maybe even a lifetime) dieting, food is a highly charged issue. Food has taken on categories such as legal or illegal, good or evil, low-fat or high-fat, no-calories or lots-of-calories, on-the-list or off-the-list. Food has lost its basic meaning: that which we eat for nourishment and pleasure. Food is not good or bad. Food is just food. How can you get to a place of eating naturally, healthfully, pleasurably? Stop dieting. Legalize every food. Begin listening to what your body needs and wants. Learn to enjoy food and eating once again. When you sit down to dinner, stop the battle going on in your head. Get back to basics: food = nourishment; eating = pleasure.

affirmation

Today I choose what and when to eat.

size-wise action

If you're having trouble tuning into your hunger today, remind yourself that food is not your enemy. Food is just food. Feel your hunger. Ask your body what it wants. Then sit down and enjoy your meal. No muss. No fuss. No guilt.

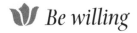 *Be willing*

Body-size acceptance can happen to you, but first you must be willing. It is necessary to be willing because only then are you giving yourself a choice. It's no longer "I can" or "I can't." It becomes a matter of "I'm willing" or "I'm not willing." Activating your will has nothing to do with will-power. Activating your will has everything to do with opening yourself to the energy to make a decision. Just say you are willing to accept and care for your body. Watch how your energy moves your decisions toward living large. You'll see that this is not a struggle like dieting; rather, it's like opening a window of change. Become willing to open the windows of your mind and body, letting the fresh breeze of acceptance blow through your life.

affirmation

Today I am willing to accept and care for my body.

size-wise action

Whenever you face a decision of any kind, practice asking, "Am I willing?" Listen for your answer. Notice how things become easier when you are willing to do them. Build a bridge from this learning to your process of body-size acceptance.

🌷 *Reframing*

Reframing is a word therapists use to describe a technique in which we take an idea that we see in one way and change it by changing our perception (or frame) of it to enhance our purposes. Reframing is an effective way to change the culturally negative messages about weight into personally positive messages. For instance, instead of "exercise for weight loss" (drudgery), we think "movement for pleasure" (fun). Or instead of "fat and unhealthy" (bad), we think "being big means being strong" (good). Or we reframe "fat and unlovable" (isolating) into "large, soft, cuddly, warm" (supportive). Reframing takes very little energy, just creative thinking. It's easier to change the frame than to repaint the picture.

affirmation

Today I am willing to change my perception of myself.

size-wise action

Imagine that your thoughts are a frame around the picture of your life. Change the way the picture looks by changing the frame. Write about this in your journal.

❧ *Swap stories*

It's hard to think of size acceptance as an individual process, as unique as the woman who is going through it. But it is. That doesn't mean, however, that sharing our experiences is futile. It isn't. In fact, swapping stories is a very powerful way to heal ourselves and others of the pain of living in nonconforming bodies. We may not be living our size-accepting lives exactly alike, in lockstep, as if there were a recipe to follow. But if you *are* learning to live with yourself in the body you already have, when someone asks *how*, tell her your story (but don't give advice or say you've found the only way). Then ask that person to tell you her story. Swap stories. Proudly witness each other's individual, unique, creative process.

affirmation

I freely share my experiences of body-size acceptance with other women.

size-wise action

Gather several of your friends who are interested in exploring their issues of body-size acceptance. Set the ground rules: no advice; just listen. If it feels good, meet again.

❦ *See the world as large as it is*

Paradoxically, larger women are encouraged to have smaller lives—lives confined to dieting and body-hate, to little risk-taking and much fear, guilt, and shame. Having to face a seemingly hostile world makes it hard to get out of the house on some days. But your life does not have to be small if you are large. Be willing to live a life larger than your body. Learn to see the world through your size, not in spite of it. How? By remembering that the world is a place big enough for you. There is room for your ample body, your spacious mind, your colorful emotions, abundant creativity, and open heart. A cosmos exists out there, a universe larger than your body. There is room for you.

affirmation

My world is as large as I am willing to make it.

size-wise action

Find a picture of the universe, complete with galaxies. Locate the Milky Way and then the Earth. See how small Earth is in relation to the rest of the cosmos? Think about how small you are in relation to that! Write about this perspective of "right proportion" in your journal.

Thin women have problems, too

Psychological theories about fat people abound. For example, some therapists believe that *all* fat women have eating disorders, and/or were sexually abused, and/or are angry and depressed. These therapists really believe that a person has to be thin to be psychologically and emotionally healthy. This is a lie. Theories are just that: theories. They have never been proved by research. The truth is that some fat people have these problems, but so do some thin people. So if you find yourself blaming all your problems on your weight, stop. Or if your therapist tries to pigeonhole you into one of the above theories, educate your therapist. Find the solutions to your problems by putting your weight in this perspective: is my weight the problem or is weight society's problem?

affirmation

Accepting my size is my personal solution to society's weight problem.

size-wise action

If you have problems, imagine how you can solve them without first going on a diet. Remind yourself that our fat-phobic culture, not your size, may be the culprit.

❦ Size acceptance is a healthy response to a pathological culture

Size diversity means just that: people come in a variety of sizes and shapes, just as they differ in color, nationality, race, and ethnicity. If the world believed in size diversity we would not have the "sizism" and fat phobia we see today. But the world doesn't believe in size diversity, so those of us who are outside of cultural acceptability must find ways to live healthfully in a toxic environment. There are many ways that take us to the same conclusion: size acceptance leads to better self-care, improved self-esteem, and a better quality of life. What worthier goal could we embrace? Rethink your body size. See it in relation to the rest of the bodies in the world, in the beautiful spectrum of diversity of human beings.

affirmation

I accept all of me.

size-wise action

The next time you are in a gathering, notice all the kinds of bodies present. Do any two look alike? Reflect on this and write about it in your journal.

❦ "I feel fat" really means "I feel bad"

In this culture women feel a lot of shame about their bodies. We feel that our bodies are bad, just by their nature. This is because there is an enormous gap between a woman's actual body and her "ideal" body. We forget, however, that our "ideal" body is created by the culture and may not be the body we would choose for ourselves without cultural pressure. One shorthand way in which women have learned to express their shame is to say "I feel fat" when we really mean "I feel bad." Correct this faulty expression by remembering that being a fat person does not equal being a bad person. Say what you mean. Mean what you say. If you feel bad, say so-and keep your body out of it!

affirmation

I say what I mean and mean what I say.

size-wise action

Every time you hear yourself saying, "I feel fat," stop and ask yourself how you really feel. Write about this in your journal as a way of keeping track of your emotions. Then work out these emotions in some way other than by deflecting them onto your body.

Part 4

live large!

🌷 *Live large!*

Life is made up of many things—many kinds of people, places, experiences, ideas, creations. In fact, life is a huge palette of colors, textures, tastes, and sounds. Life is large because *it has to be!* Life has to make room for the infinite variety of creation. If it's okay for life to be *large*, then why is it *not* okay for us to be large? Stop your negative judgments about your body. Start seeing your large body as an extension of your expansive mind and spacious spirit. Large body, large mind, large spirit. LARGE LIFE!

affirmation

I am large in body, mind, and spirit.

size-wise action

Think of ways in which you can expand your mind. Think of ways in which you can give space for your spirit to grow. Put these thoughts in your journal and add to them whenever you can. Make a commitment to do these things as often as possible, and watch yourself live large!

🌱 *Trust yourself*

Do you find that you rely on others to tell you how you should think about something, feel about something, behave about something? Do you look under every rock and in every corner for the right answers to your life's problems? Seeking answers outside yourself diminishes your ability to build trust in your own perceptions, experiences, and intellect. This is behavior doomed to keep you dependent on everyone else's opinion of who you are. From this moment on, dare to live your life with a trusting attitude about yourself, your perceptions, your value as a woman of size—even if the rest of the world sees you differently.

affirmation
I trust my perceptions and experiences.

size-wise action
Go back in memory to those times when you made decisions on your own that turned out great. Write these down. The next time you have to decide something, trust yourself to make the right decision. If you are having a hard time doing so, take out your list, read it, and remember to trust yourself.

 *Activism*

The word *activism* has been turning people off since the 1960s. It conjures up images of picket lines, angry people, burning bras. *Activism* also has another meaning: commitment. Activism changes the world, which means that activists are agents of change. If you are living in a larger body, then becoming an activist can be a good thing. This doesn't have to be a big deal. It can mean writing a letter to a TV station that shows positive (or negative) images of larger people. It can mean joining a size-acceptance organization or mentoring a woman who is just beginning to accept her body. Rethink the role of activism in your life. You can change the world one action at a time!

affirmation

I am active in promoting size acceptance for everyone.

size-wise action

Choose one of the items mentioned above (or think of one your own) as a way of becoming active in the process of size acceptance.

❦ Feed the hungry people of the world instead of the bank accounts of the diet industry

Spending your money on diets is ineffective because diets have a 95 percent failure rate. Would you seriously consider spending money on anything else that would break or fall apart 95 percent of the time? I doubt it! But we are seduced over and over again by the promise that *this* diet will be the one that will finally make us thin and keep us thin forever. Think of all the starving people we could feed with the money we spend on diets. Around the world, one million people starve to death each week. In that same seven-day period, Americans spend $600 million on diet products. That's enough to provide $600 worth of food for each of those starving people. Think about those numbers the next time you are tempted to spend your money on a diet.

affirmation

I spend my money on things that make a difference.

size-wise action

When you are tempted to go on a diet, write a check to your local food pantry or another organization that feeds the hungry. They need the money more than the diet industry does.

🌷 *Find your voice*

Because you live in a larger body, do you find yourself thinking that you don't have a right to speak up? Do you disregard yourself, your inner voice, your intuitions and experiences because of the shame you might feel about being over the height-weight charts? Have you been silenced by doctors, therapists, teachers, even strangers on the street? Well, the time to stop being silenced is *now*. You have a voice. Find it. Use it to speak your truth about being a woman of size. Use it to silence people who intentionally or unintentionally shame you. You don't have to be silent any longer. You're allowed to speak up for yourself, regardless of your size.

affirmation

I speak my truth about my body.

size-wise action

Think of a situation in which you lost your voice. Go back and relive that situation, imagining that you used your strong voice instead. What would you say? How would you say it? Remember that scenario the next time you find yourself speechless because of shame.

 *Purpose*

Having a purpose is a wonderful place to be. Being directed by our purpose in life means knowing what is important to us and then doing the things that have meaning for us. This may be our job or our career. It may have something to do with our families. It may be about our creativity expressed in a myriad of ways. Living with our purpose centered in our thoughts and actions is valuable for larger women because it puts our purpose first and our bodies someplace after that. It means that we can focus our attention and energy on things that matter in the world for ourselves and others, regardless of our body size. Living with purpose is the best way to live.

affirmation

I know what is important for me to do, and I do it.

size-wise action

Have you given any thought to what your purpose is in life? If you haven't, the time to start is now. What special gifts, talents, creativity, and interest have you been given to use for the betterment of yourself and society? Discover them. Use them.

❦ Eating habits change as we go through the process of body-size acceptance

If food has ever been a problem for you, your personal process of body-size acceptance will probably include normalizing your relationship with it. Food is usually (but not always) a problem for women of all sizes because of our complex relationship with it: we are expected to buy it, prepare it, serve it, clean up after it is eaten, but not eat it ourselves. In addition, there is enormous pressure to diet, whether we are thin or fat. If food has been a problem for you, I have good news: once you begin the process of body-size acceptance, which includes the decision to stop dieting for weight loss, you will automatically improve your relationship with food. So commit to a nondieting, size-acceptance lifestyle and watch your relationship with food become what it should be: normal and natural.

affirmation

I have a normal, natural relationship with food.

size-wise action

Do you need help in establishing a nondieting lifestyle? Use the "food pyramid" developed by the American Dietetic Association as a model for eating healthfully.

♥ *"Obese" is a misguided way to say "fat"*

The word *obese* has a negative connotation. It comes from the Latin word *obedere*, which means "to eat away"— a faulty assumption. Health-care practitioners and researchers use the word *obese* to describe a severe medical condition, a disease. At one time this definition was applied to people at the extreme of the human weight range—a mere .05 percent of the population. Now the definition is used to refer to anyone who is 20 percent over the height-weight charts—a liberal use of the word, indeed. Let's face it, if the word *obese* has been misnamed, misdefined, and misused by almost everyone, why use it?

affirmation

I am a fat woman.

size-wise action

Try using a word other than *obese* to describe a fat person. Try using the word *fat* until you become comfortable with it.

❦ The word "overweight" means nothing

Overweight has been overused. In fact, the word means nothing at all. Being overweight is a relative condition, relative to *what* weight or *whose* weight. The height-weight charts are the basis for this term. Since they were created in the 1940s, the height-weight charts have been the standard by which the insurance industry classifies its policyholders as either the "ideal" (not average) weight or over that "ideal." The medical community has adopted these charts as a measure of who is healthy: people in the "ideal" weight range. Anyone over the ideal is "overweight," hence automatically unhealthy. If you understand how and why the height-weight charts were developed, you will think differently about them as an indicator of your healthy weight. Overweight? I ask, how can you be *over* your own weight?

affirmation

My weight is perfect for me.

size-wise action

Learn about the height-weight charts. Read *Never Too Thin: Why Women Are at War with Their Bodies*, by Roberta Pollak Seid, or *Big Fat Lies: The Truth About Your Health and Your Weight*, by Glenn Gaesser. They will open your eyes.

♥ *Discipline*

Diet gurus tell us that to be successful in losing weight we must be disciplined—disciplined enough to say "no" to forbidden foods, disciplined enough to exercise several hours a day, disciplined enough to deny ourselves pleasure through eating. If we haven't been successful in losing weight permanently, the problem isn't that we lack discipline. The problem is that diets don't work. Don't buy into the idea that you aren't good or lack discipline. Buy into the idea that you have been disciplined (good) in other places in your life, places where you reap *permanent* rewards. We have lost weight. So what? What else have we done that shows our true measure of discipline?

affirmation

I practice discipline in appropriate areas of my life.

size-wise action

Make a list of everything you have disciplined yourself to accomplish. A successful image? An education? A top-notch career? A healthy body? Put the list up in a place where it can frequently remind you that you do have the gumption to do what's important.

 *Nurturance*

Women are really big on nurturing others—taking care of everybody and everything except themselves. Larger women have a tendency to do even more nurturing than the average woman. Sometimes we do this because we are seen as "earth mothers." But more often it is because we are trying, perhaps unconsciously, to make up for the perceived inadequacy of our bodies by being *overly* adequate everywhere else. Don't fall into the trap of taking care of everyone and everything because you feel bad about your body. Nurture yourself first. Ask for nurturance from others. When you feel that *you* are being taken care of, you will be better able to nurture others in an appropriate, affirming way.

affirmation

Today I nurture myself in as many ways as possible.

size-wise action

Look at an average day in your life. How much time do you spend taking care of others' needs? Balance the time, putting you first on your list. What can you do today to nurture yourself?

Yes!

How often do you tell yourself *no* just because you're fat? *No* to buying comfortable, well-fitting clothes. *No* to getting regular physicals. *No* to swimming or walking or some other enjoyable way to move. *No* to relationships. *No* to career or job changes. *No* to going back to school. *No* to moving to a more desirable location. Say *no* to *no*! And start saying *yes* to life! Yes, I deserve beautiful clothes. Yes, I deserve to take care of my health. Yes, I deserve to buy a bathing suit and go to the beach. Yes, I deserve good friends. Yes, I deserve a new, better-paying job. Yes, I deserve to expand my intellect. Yes, I deserve to live where I want. Get the picture? You deserve to have the life you want in the body you already have. Just say *yes*!

affirmation

Today I say *yes* to life in every possible way.

size-wise action

Think of one thing you've been saying *no* to because of your weight. Rethink this. Say, "I deserve it." Then go do it.

 Hunger

Needing to eat is as natural as needing to breathe. It's what makes us fully alive, what sustains us. Breathing only requires air to be satisfied, whereas we have a myriad of choices when it comes to satisfying our hunger. In our culture, hunger is more than a physical need—eating is also a source of pleasure and, for some women, pain. How did a natural function come to bring so much grief to so many women? The answers include dieting, food restriction, fear of getting fat, and fear of being seen as physically imperfect in a culture that values us primarily for our appearance. These add up to women having a crazy and complicated relationship with food and hunger. There is a way out of all this. Remind yourself that eating can be as natural as breathing.

affirmation

I am capable of responding to my hunger in healthful and pleasurable ways.

size-wise action

Allow yourself to feel hungry. Begin to learn what you're hungry for. Experiment with different kinds of foods without categorizing them as "bad" or "good." Eat without guilt. Learn to enjoy food once again.

 *Fitness*

Watch TV commercials and you'd think that fitness is only for the thin, young, and beautiful. It's not! Fitness is for everybody in every body. Being fit is your right as well as the right of the woman wearing a thong leotard. What are you waiting for? Begin to think of fitness as your entitlement. Throw out your old ideas about moving your body—you know, the go-for-the-burn mentality. Do any or all of the following: put on various types of music and move to the rhythms; walk through the woods, on the beach, or in your neighborhood; skip rope; climb up and down steps; garden; park your car farther away from your home or office. All of these activities can help you become fitter, even if you are fat.

affirmation

I am a fat and fit woman.

size-wise action

If you need the inspiration to begin moving, read *Great Shape: The First Fitness Guide for Large Women*, by Pat Lyons and Debby Burgard.

❦ *Become a size-wise woman*

Wisdom is a sacred thing. It comes out of our ability to "compost" our experiences into a rich soil in which our selves can grow. Wisdom comes from living fully, from reflecting, from listening to our intuitions, from trusting our inner voice, from acting on our internal "wise woman." When it comes to our bodies, it is hard for women to act wisely on a regular basis. That's because our body wisdom has been overshadowed by external authorities—doctors, the insurance industry, fashion designers, obesity researchers, pharmaceutical companies—all of whom have an economic interest in leading us to distrust our body wisdom. So how can you become a size-wise woman? Stop listening to everyone else and start listening to your body. It's wiser than you think.

affirmation

I use my wisdom in making decisions about my body.

size-wise action

Do you know a wise woman? How does she feel about her body? Ask her to share some of her body wisdom with you. And begin to listen to your own body, respecting its wise messages.

 *Pleasure*

In our puritanical culture the word *pleasure* has acquired a rotten reputation. Pleasure brings up pictures of decadence, selfishness, indulgence, hedonism. To the contrary, pleasure is a good thing! In fact, it's *great* to give yourself pleasure in as many ways as you can imagine. Why? Why not? Why deny yourself enjoyment, delight, or joy? Giving yourself pleasure does not mean you will become selfish and forget about everyone else's needs. Giving yourself pleasure means that you have put yourself on your own list of people to take care of. So take pleasure out of the back reaches of your mind. Dust it off. Think of ways to delight yourself today. It can be anything that brings a smile to your face, a twinkle to your eye, a tingle to your body, a light to your soul.

affirmation

I am entitled to be pleasured in any way I want.

size-wise action

If you can't think of ways to give yourself pleasure, here are a few ideas: get a massage, make time for reading, go dancing, have lunch with your best friend, buy a great new outfit, take a hot bath, hug someone, smile.

 *Sensuality*

What does it mean to be *sensual?* Saying the word conjures up images of being physical: of feeling ourselves through our sense of touch, covering our skin with satin and silk; of delighting our eyes with color, softness, and curvaceousness; of pleasuring our ears with music that inspires us to move with feeling; of tingling our taste buds with creamy, melt-in-your-mouth foods; of surprising our noses with delicious fragrances. Sensual women know how to delight themselves and others through the five senses. Sensual women come in all sizes. In fact, sensuality comes much easier for woman of size because our bodies are larger, softer, curvier, smoother. There's more to touch, more to hold, more to feel, more to delight and surprise. By nature's design, a larger woman is a sensual woman.

affirmation

I am a sensual woman.

size-wise action

Heighten your sensuality by wearing fabrics that feel good on your body, look good on your body, and move with your body. Find someone who will help dress you as the sensual woman you were born to be.

 *Sexuality*

Sex is a complicated matter for everyone in this crazy world, but it is especially so for larger women. Because we are constantly barraged with images of who is supposed to be sexy (women with "perfect" bodies), we are made to feel left out because of our size. Many larger women deny themselves the pleasure of feeling sexy, of looking sexy, of being sexy. They think that having a sexual relationship is outside their realm. Not true. If you're alive, you have a right to behave in a sexual way, to get your sexual needs met, regardless of your size. So think of yourself as a sexy woman. Sexuality is a state of mind; it's not about the size of a body.

affirmation

I am a sexual woman.

size-wise action

Many people prefer larger women as sexual partners because of our softness, roundness, and fullness. Think of your sexuality as a beacon of light designed to attract those who prefer your body type. Write about this in your journal.

⚜ *Be gentle with yourself*

It's easy to be harsh and critical with ourselves, judging everything we do. It's easy because we have internalized the negative voice of the culture that says we are never good enough, never creative enough, never rich enough, and, of course, never *thin* enough. In fact, we're never enough, period! It's time to shut off that negative, nagging voice that relentlessly pursues us from dawn to dusk. What we can do, instead, is replace the critical voice with the voice of gentleness. No, we aren't perfect. But who is? Be gentle with yourself. Talk to yourself with patience, care, and kindness. Treat yourself as if you were the most valuable, precious jewel on earth, because you are!

affirmation

I treat myself with gentleness.

size-wise action

Take on your critical voice. Dialogue with it in your journal. Tell it to be quiet or you will lock it away in some closet of your mind forever. Now befriend your gentle voice. Become familiar with what it has to say to you. Write these things in your journal.

❦ *Reclaim your body*

When was the last time you *really* paid attention to your body? And I don't mean policing what you feed it or flogging it with go-for-the-burn exercise. Reclaim your body in other ways: Touch yourself. Notice where you feel bones, muscle, fat, softness, hardness, roughness, smoothness. Examine each finger and toe, the length of your arm, the stretch of your leg. Discover the wonder of your belly and thighs and breasts. What do you notice about your body when you are standing, sitting, lying down? Hug yourself. Look at yourself as if you were seeing your body for the first time. Create a sense of discovery about your body: feel it, look at it, be in it *without judgment*. Your body is uniquely yours, a gift.

affirmation
My body belongs to me.

size-wise action
Pay attention to your negative, judgmental voice. Lock it up, put a muzzle on it, silence it. Ask yourself what your life would be like if you never passed judgment on your body. Write about the above exercise in your journal.

❦ *Dieting steals time*

Besides costing way too much money, dieting also takes its toll on our time. If you don't believe this, ask yourself how much time you've *already spent* today wondering and worrying about what you are or are not going to eat, when you should eat, even *if* you should eat! Multiply that by every day that you have been conscious of restraining your eating (dieting). That amounts to a lot of time! Ask yourself this: what will I do with all the time I'll have when I've stopped dieting? Think about it. What will replace thinking about food and eating, preparing special meals, going to weight-loss clinics for weigh-ins and meetings, talking about the newest diets with your friends, reading about the latest miracle cure for fat? When you stop dieting, what will you do with all your time?

affirmation

I spend my time wisely.

size-wise action

Keep asking yourself what you really want to do with your precious time. Write about these things. Begin doing them as a way to replace dieting and food-obsessive behavior.

🌷 *Move your body*

Move your body for the most important reason of all: it's designed to move! It has muscles and joints that enable us to do simple things like moving a finger and complex things like swimming and dancing. Remember when you were a girl and you played hopscotch and tag, jumped rope, ran down the block? Remember the freedom that came with *not thinking* about your body, but *just moving* your body? You can feel that freedom and aliveness today. Just move your body. Move it in any way that pleasures you, just as you did when you were a kid. It doesn't have to be a step-aerobics class, or jogging, or speed-walking, or lifting weights (unless you really want to do these things). It can be as free and simple as walking the dog, gardening, or dancing to your favorite music. Come alive! Move!

affirmation

I feel most alive when I move my body.

size-wise action

Pick an enjoyable way to move your body. Try different things. Move your body because it feels good.

 *Medical care*

For a larger woman, going to the doctor's office can be incredibly scary and painful—and not just because we're sick, but because we're fat. If we need medical attention for something physical, we know that the doctor will most likely focus on our weight as the cause of any ailment from a sore throat to cancer. Add to that being weighed as soon as we come in, and the difficulty of trying to keep our dignity while our body is hanging out of a too-small paper robe and we are sitting in a too-small chair. No wonder fat people avoid the doctor! Remember: you are entitled to good medical care. Go to the doctor for an examination when you need one, or for your routine medical care. Assert your right to take care of your body medically.

affirmation

I am entitled to medical care for my body.

size-wise action

Find a size-friendly physician. They are out there! Refuse to be weighed for routine checkups. Ask for a bigger robe or two robes, without shame. Practice doing this with a friend before you go to the doctor.

❦ Heal the past by letting go of the hurts

Whether you grew up in a larger body or have more recently become a woman of size, it's hard to forget being hurt because of your body size. It sometimes seems that everyone is intentionally or unintentionally shaming us about size—in ways that range from providing seats that are too small to denying us positive portrayals in the media. It hurts to be fat in this culture, and it's difficult not to be angry at those who have shamed us. Yet we must move on, past the anger and hurt. We must realize that this is a societal problem, one that we can help change by changing our attitudes about ourselves and other people of size. We can turn our anger into creative energy. Move on by letting go of the hurt. Move on by healing the past.

affirmation

I am willing to let go of my past hurts about my body.

size-wise action

Write down all the ways you've been hurt because of your size. Then perform a letting-go ritual by burning the paper, saying that you let go of your past hurts and are now open to new direction and energy in your life as a proud woman of size.

 *Self-talk*

I f we monitor what we say to ourselves about ourselves, we often find that our self-talk is filled with criticism and negativity. This negative self-talk has far-reaching effects, not only on our self-esteem but also on our physical health. Every time we say something negative in our self-talk, we are assaulting our *body* as well as our minds and emotions. The body responds to this negativity by creating discomfort and disease. Remember, your body hears what you say to it. Create comfort and health by talking kindly and gently to yourself about your body.

affirmation

I talk to myself with caring and kindness.

size-wise action

Monitor your self-talk about your body. Every time you find yourself thinking or saying something disparaging, stop. Remember that you are assaulting your body. Say something gentle to yourself instead.

 *Comfort*

Being a bigger woman brings its share of discomfort in this fat-phobic world, so we have to do whatever we can to introduce comfort into our lives on a regular basis. Increase your physical comfort by examining your home, car, and workplace and replacing things that are not comfortable with things that are. Buy larger or armless chairs. Get a seat-belt extender for your car or for airplane travel. Choose clothes for comfort and style. Stop being uncomfortable in your larger body! Go for comfort.

affirmation

I am comfortable in my body.

size-wise action

If you feel uncomfortable in your larger body, consider following the suggestions above, one comfortable change at a time.

Love

Love is the most wonderful emotion in which to bathe ourselves. Unfortunately, it is an emotion that many larger women don't allow themselves to feel for themselves or to accept from others. Our size can get in the way of letting love in. Maybe you do have a hard time loving yourself because of your body, but don't let yourself get in the way of allowing others to love you, regardless. Let the lovers of you love you. Let them touch you, get inside you, admire you. Let them teach you how to love yourself in the body you already have. Let them love you until you can love yourself.

affirmation

I am a loving and lovable woman.

size-wise action

Who really loves you? Spend lots of time with those people. Ask them why they love you. Remember their words when you are about to assault yourself with negative body-talk. Watch how they love you, and practice treating yourself the same way.

 Clothing

When it comes to clothing, larger women learned a different set of rules than the rest of the world. Our rules included such things as never wear horizontal stripes or bright colors; never tuck in your blouse or shirt; never wear a belt; never wear shorts in public; and never own a bathing suit, let alone wear one. And we thought we always had to buy an article of clothing just because it fit, instead of because we really liked it. Well, throw away your old ideas about clothing. And while you're at it, throw away any clothes in your closet that don't fit you today or that you don't like or feel comfortable in. Then go to a quality larger women's specialty shop and ask someone to dress you, to help you find clothes that are right for your type of body. Spend your money on quality, comfortable, stylish clothes. You're worth it!

affirmation

I deserve to have quality, comfortable, stylish clothing.

size-wise action

Allow yourself the luxury of a shopping spree in a quality women's clothing shop. Yes, the clothes might cost more, but so what? Dress yourself with pride.

🌱 *Learn from the innocence of babies*

As we grow older we grow wiser about many things. With age, though, we tend to forget some of the things that once came naturally to us—like eating when we're hungry, sleeping when we're tired, and crying when we feel bad or uncomfortable. If your responses to your needs for food, sleep, or comfort are out of sync, take a moment to learn from the innocence of babies. Watch how they respond naturally to their needs. Remember that you used to know those things, but you unlearned them as you became socialized, as you put on the culture's filters concerning how you "should" be. Babies may not know a lot about life, but they have an innate wisdom about living. Respond to your needs in an innocent way: eat when you're hungry; sleep when you're tired; cry when you feel emotionally distraught.

affirmation

I respond to my needs in a natural, loving way.

size-wise action

Write in your journal about what you have learned from watching a baby. Practice that behavior as often as possible.

 *Compassion*

It's easy to become jealous of our thinner sisters. When we look at them we might think that because they are thin they have the perfect job, the perfect relationship, the perfect life. We imagine that they have no body-image concerns, that they can dress any way they like, that they are healthy and happy. These are fantasies. Thinner women have problems. They have body-image concerns. They are not always happy or healthy. In fact, it is a rare woman in this culture who is perfectly content with her body. It doesn't matter if a woman is thin; she hears the same messages that you hear—get thinner! Practice compassion for all women, thin or fat. As long as we live in this culture, we're all in the same body-image boat, regardless of our size

affirmation

I show compassion toward all women, regardless of size.

size-wise action

Ask a thinner friend how she feels about her body. Share your experience of living in a larger body. Make a bridge between her experience and yours by practicing compassion.

❧ *Live your perfect life*

Entertain this fantasy: You are living your perfect life in your ideal body. When you wake up in the morning you feel excited about the day's possibilities. You look in the mirror and smile at your reflection before getting into the shower. While bathing, you notice how good your body feels, how smooth and soft. When you go to your closet, you find an array of beautiful, comfortable clothing and put on what is perfect for your day's activities. You have a breakfast of healthful, nourishing, and pleasurable foods. You go to a job that provides you with satisfaction as well as money. Friends meet you for dinner at a wonderful restaurant, and you go home tired but fulfilled by your day. You sleep soundly, dreaming of what's important. This life, this perfect life, can be yours in the body you already have. It doesn't require you to lose weight or to be a size you aren't. Now go live your perfect day.

affirmation

My life is the perfect life for me.

size-wise action

Make your fantasy life come true one action at a time. Write in your journal about how you can do this.

❦ *Abundant living in an abundant body*

*A*bundance is a very good word. It means having a great or plentiful amount of something, a fullness to overflowing, ampleness, wealth. Having an abundant life can be much like having an abundant body: being plentiful, ample, full. Celebrate your abundant body by living an abundant life—a life full of creativity, joy, peacefulness, and love. Overflow with all the good things. Allow your larger body to symbolize all that is larger in your life, all that is abundant, so that when you look in the mirror you can smile and know that the size of your body matches the size of your life!

affirmation

I live my life with celebration and abundance!

size-wise action

Celebrate the size of your body by going out and doing something big, something that reflects your big body, big heart, and big life. Celebrate your abundance!

 *Resources*

Books

Body Image

Cooke, Kaz. *Real Gorgeous: The Truth About Body and Beauty.* WW Norton & Company, 1998.

Hutchinson, Marcia. *Transforming Body Image: Learning to Love the Body You Have.* Ten Speed/The Crossing Press, 1985.

Hutchinson, Marcia. *200 Ways to Love the Body You Have.* Ten Speed/ The Crossing Press, 1999.

Kilbourne, Jeanne. *Can't Buy My Love: How Advertising Changes the Way We Think and Feel.* Touchstone Books, 1999.

The Melpomene Institute for Women's Research. *The Bodywise Woman.* Prentice-Hall, 1992.

Wolf, Naomi. *The Beauty Myth: How Images of Beauty Are Used Against Women.* William Morrow, 1991.

Health at Every Size (HAES)

Bennett, William and Gurin, Joel. *The Dieter's Dilemma.* Basic Books, 1982.

Bliss, Kelly. *Don't Weight: Get Moving and Eat Healthy Now.* Xlibris Corporation, 2001.

Fraser, Laura. *Losing It: False Hopes and Fat Profits in the Diet Industry.* Plume, 1998.

Gaesser, Glenn. *Big Fat Lies: The Truth About Your Weight and Your Health*. Gürze Books, 2002.

Hirschman, Jane and Munter, Carol. *Overcoming Overeating*. Fawcett Columbine, 1988.

Hirschman, Jane and Munter, Carol. *When Women Stop Hating Their Bodies*. Ballantine, 1995.

Kratina, Karin, Nancy L. King and Dayle Hayes. *Moving Away From Diets: New Ways to Heal Eating Problems and Exercise Resistance*. Helm Seminars, 1996.

Lyons, Pat and Burgard, Debora. *Great Shape: The First Fitness Guide for Large Women*. iUniverse.com, 2000.

Mundy, Alicia. *Dispensing With the Truth: The Victims, the Drug Companies, and the Dramatic Story Behind the Battle Over Fen-Phen*. St. Martin's Press, 2001.

Omichinski, Linda. *You Count, Calories Don't*. Hyperion, 1992.

Rice, Rochelle. *Real Fitness for Real Women: A Unique Workout Program for the Plus-Size Woman*. Warner Books, 2001.

Satter, Ellyn. *Secrets of Feeding a Healthy Family*. Kelcey Press, 1999.

History of Women's Body Image, Fat and Weight

Seid, Roberta Pollack. *Never Too Thin: Why Women Are At War With Their Bodies*. Prentice-Hall, 1989.

Schwartz, Hillel. *Never Satisfied: A Cultural History of Diets, Fantasies and Fat*. The Free Press, 1986.

Psychological Health

Estes, Clarissa Pinkola. *Women Who Run With the Wolves: Myths and Stories of the Wild Woman Archetype.* Ballantine, 1992.

Ferrucci, Piero. *What We May Be: Techniques for Psychological and Spiritual Growth Through Psychosynthesis.* Jeremy Tarcher, 1982.

Size-Acceptance

Bernell, Bonnie. *Bountiful Women: Large Women's Secrets for Living the Life They Desire.* Wild Canyon Press, 2000.

Bruno, Barbara. *Worth Your Weight: What You Can Do About a Weight Problem.* Rutledge Books, 1996.

Erdman, Cheri. *Nothing to Lose: A Guide to Sane Living in a Larger Body.* HarperSanFrancisco, 1995.

Goodman, Charisse. *The Invisible Woman: Confronting Weight Prejudice in America.* Gürze Books, 1995.

Johnson, Carol. *Self-Esteem Comes In All Sizes: Healthy and Happy At Your Natural Weight.* Gürze Books, 2001.

Manheim, Camryn. *Wake Up, I'm Fat!* Broadway Books, 1999.

Mayer, Ken. *Real Women Don't Diet! One Man's Praise of Large Women and His Outrage at the Society That rejects Them.* Bartleby Press, 1993.

Poulton, Terry. *No Fat Chicks: How Women Are Brainwashed to Hate Their Bodies and Spend Their Money.* Key Porter Books, 1996.

Roberts, Nancy. *Breaking All the Rules: Feeling Good and Looking Great No Matter What Your Size.* Penguin Books, 1985.

Schoenfielder, Lisa and Weiser, Barb. *Shadow on a Tightrope: Writings by Women on Fat Liberation.* Aunt Lute Press, 1983.

Solovay, Sandra. *Tipping the Scales of Justice: Fighting Weight-Based Discrimination.* Prometheus Books, 2000

Sullivan, Judy. *Size Wise: A Catalog of More Than 1000 Resources for Living with Confidence and Comfort at Any Size.* Avon, 1997.

Wann, Marilyn. *Fat!So? Because You Do Not Have to Apologize for Your Size.* Ten Speed Press, 1999.

Wiley, Carol. *Journeys to Self-Acceptance: Fat Women Speak.* The Crossing Press, 1994.

Organizations, Magazines and Websites

Abundia Retreats for Larger Women
Contact Barbara Spaulding
847-705-9256

Amplestuff & Ample Shopper
914-679-3316
www.amplestuff.com

Big Beautiful Woman (BBW) Magazine On-Line
www.bbwmagazine.com

Body Positive
Boosting body image at any weight
www.bodypositive.com

The Body Positive
Videos exploring weight and eating disorders
www.thebodypositive.org

Chicago Center for Overcoming Overeating
PO Box 48
Deerfield, IL 60015
708-853-1200

Council on Size and Weight Discrimination
www.cswd.org

Fat Chance (video)
Bullfrog Films
1-800-543-3764

Feeling Good Fitness
www.feelinggoodfitness.com

Fitness and Healthy Living with Bliss
www.kellybliss.com
Healthy Weight Network
www.healthyweightnetwork.com

Holistic Health Promotion/Health At Every Size (HAES)
Contact Jonathan Robison, Ph.D.
www.jonrobison.net

Junonia Active Wear for Sizes 14 and Up
1-800-JUNONIA
www.junonia.com

Largely Positive, Inc.
www.largelypositive.com

Largesse, the Network for Size Esteem
www.eskimo.com/largesse

National Association to Advance Fat Acceptance (NAAFA)
916-558-6880
www.naafa.org

National Center for Overcoming Overeating
www.overcomingovereating.com

Radiance Magazine Online
www.radiancemagazine.com

Size Wise
www.sizewise.com

❦ *Acknowledgments*

To my parents, Bill and Dolores, for believing in me and always being there when I need them. To my soul brother, Patrick, for loving me BIG time. To my brother, Michael, for understanding a "big body" mentality from a male point of view. To my brother, Christopher, for his optimism and faith. To my brother, Bill, for never tiring of listening to me ramble on about everything and anything, and for being my head cheerleader.

To my smart and beautiful nieces, Nicole, Erin and Kristen, whom I love very much.

To my eclectic group of faithful friends and cheerleaders: Bob Berger, Les Borzy, Sarah and Benoit Delcourt, Jeff and Betsy Edwards, Joyce and David Fletcher, MJ Hartwell, Lorin Katz, Vicki Knauerhase, Jeannie Kokes, Vicki Koutavas, Nancy Lenz, Marilyn and George Marchetti, Lois Neville, Carol Petok, David and Marcia Rigg, Barbara Robinette and David Kolberg, Jon Robison, Mary Gayle Selfridge, Art Snedeker, Dorothy Squitieri and Judy Sullivan.

To Pat Lyons for being my mentor and good, good friend.

To all the women whose lives have touched mine at the Abundia retreats and in my classes and workshops - thank you for sharing your selves and your stories. I truly appreciate each and every one of you as my "sister of size". You are the reason I do this work.

To the Jones family for taking me in as one of their own: Bill, whom I dearly miss, Phyllis, Moya, Candy, Alison, Gillian, Fawn and Peregrin.

And lastly to my husband, Terry Jones, for his acceptance of ALL of me. Being married to him has been one of the greatest blessings in my life.

Index

 *About the Author*

Cheri Erdman, Ed.D. was a Professor and Counselor at the College of DuPage from 1981-2003. During that time she taught her first "Women and Body Image" class in 1982, refining it into it's current "Body Image and the Larger Woman" (it is still being taught by a colleague). She is the author of two books, Nothing to Lose: A Guide to Sane Living in a Larger Body and Live Large! , and many articles in magazines and professional journals. Dr. Erdman is a co-creator of Abundia and has organized and facilitated retreats for larger women for a decade. Over the years Dr. Erdman has spoken to hundreds of audiences of all ages, educational levels and professional affiliations on the topic of women and body image. She has been interviewed for numerous local and national media pieces including NPR, Ricki Lake, the *Chicago Tribune* and *People Magazine*. Dr. Erdman is considered to be an international expert on this topic with her books being published in French, German, Portuguese and Chinese.

Dr. Erdman lived in Downers Grove, Illinois with her husband, Terry Jones, for over 20 years. She retired early from her position at College of DuPage in the summer of 2003. Currently she and Terry are living out their fantasy of traveling around the US in their RV visiting friends and seeing the sights until they figure out what they want to do next. She can be reached by e-mail at abundia22@yahoo.com

❦ *About the publisher*

Since 1980, Gürze Books has specialized in quality information on eating disorders recovery, education, advocacy, and prevention. They also have published books on size acceptance, self-esteem, body image, and related topics. Their website (www.bulimia.com) is an Internet gateway to treatment facilities, associations, basic facts, and other eating disorders sites.

 Order Form

Live Large! is available at bookstores and libraries or may be ordered directly from Gurze Books.

The Gürze Books catalogue has more than 150 books on eating disorders and related topics, including body image, size-acceptance, self-esteem, and more. The entire catalogue and much more is available online at www.gurze.com.

___ FREE copies of the Gürze Books catalogue.

___ copies of *Live Large!*
    $12.95 each plus $2.90 each for shipping.
    Quantity discounts are available.

Name _____

Address _____

City, ST, ZIP _____

Phone _____

Gürze Books
P.O. Box 2238
Carlsbad, CA 92018
(800) 756-7533

Order online at www.gurze.com!